THE
MILKMAN*S
DAUGHTER

lessons from my life's early memories

YESENIA SEVILLA

The Milkman's Daughter
Copyright © 2025 by Yesenia Sevilla

Published by
Yesenia Sevilla
ybsevilla@gmail.com

Printed in the United States of America

A special thanks to the GSD Factor Publishing Team:
Book Coach + Editor-in-Chief: Alacia Reynolds
Cover Design: Lucas Betinardi
Interior Design: Carla Green
Cover Author Headshot: Lauren Carnahan
Interior Author Headshot: Daniel Meigs

ISBN 979-8-9999596-0-7 (paperback)
ISBN 979-8-9999596-1-4 (ebook)

*For my Alexander,
your support, strength, and love are my everything.*

*For Lauren and David,
you are my will to always be and do better—I love you!*

ABOUT THE POETRY

Throughout my life, I've always turned to language and literature as a cathartic release, whether through reading, speaking multiple languages, or writing poetry. The poems included before each chapter in this book are my original works. At the time of their creation, I had no inkling of a desire to write a book, but once I began this journey, I re-read these poems and discovered a thread connecting them to the memories I shared that can only be described as synchronicity. As you read these poems and the subsequent chapters, you should be able to see the connections between the poems and the memories, and gain further insight into the impact these experiences made on my life.

CONTENTS

The In-Between

I surrender to travel back
Searching for truth buried in many lives
My soul stretching out through time
While my body holds tight to now

Slowly my body's grip lessens
I feel heavy and weightless all at once
Behind my shuttered eyes, my mind sees only light
As my soul slips into the in-between

The warmth spreads slowly through my limbs
My cheeks catch fire as the intensity grows
Although blinded by the glow
There is no fear, no trepidation

The span of minutes—felt like a lifetime
The heaviness lifts as if every cell had carried a burden
Yet simultaneously, all the spaces inside me fill
This emptying and filling laced with silence

Quietly and slowly, I rejoin the now
Feeling both replete and weightless
This lightness of being singing, "I matter, I matter!"
What lessons await in the in-between?

March 1, 2022

INTRODUCTION

Life has been one of my greatest teachers. Her lessons have been poignant, beautiful, and sometimes cruel, but they've always been invaluable. One of those lessons is that of resilience. Like many people, I used to think resilience was simply a synonym for strength, so when I thought of my own resilience, I thought of my strength and being unbreakable. I know I'm strong. I've always known that, but life taught me that though I'm strong, I am not unbreakable. I've been broken a few times. Resilience is not about being unbreakable. It's about breaking and coming back together. Then, after having a few breaks, resilience is knowing how to bend. Life has taught me how to twist, turn, shift, and curve so that I don't have to break anymore, and I want to share a few of those lessons with you.

My purpose for writing this book is twofold. The first part of that purpose is for my own healing. The other part is because I want to help women, strong, curious, sometimes lonely women. We can have great families. We can have lots of friends or, at least, a few good ones, and engaging careers, but there can still be these nagging questions that won't leave us alone. Are we truly seen? Are we truly understood?

These questions don't form out of thin air. They start forming in our childhood. Despite all the advances women have made in society, we still seem to be socialized to expect and accept being undermined, underestimated, underpaid, and underutilized. We have so much power and potential for greatness, but we have to free ourselves from the idea that someone is coming to save us.

I want those women, and all who identify and embrace femininity and womanhood, to feel seen and connected after reading this book. There are many ways to heal, but they're not always accessible. If any part of this book can help you connect with and find some self-healing that is safe and a bit more attainable than clinical, I'd like for you to try. I hope that you will start to have little moments of comfort, knowing that you are not alone. I hope that your lingering pang of loneliness will begin to subside and be replaced with renewed power and confidence.

When you read these chapters, read them to self-reflect. Try to identify core memories and experiences of your own life that were impactful. Ask yourself how these situations helped to shape who you are and how you walk through life. Reflect on those memories, whether joyful or painful, and understand that they had to happen just as they did to make you who you are. Be proud of that person, no matter what stage of life you are in, as a result of the unique circumstances that make up your identity. My goal in sharing my experiences in this way is to show that the things I've been through, good and bad, made me who I am. I like who I am, so I can share these experiences without shame or regret. I hope that after reading this, you can feel the same way.

Finally, it is important to note that the stories I share in this book are evidence of my ability to reflect. They are my experiences as I remember them, many of which happened to me in early childhood, some of which are traumatic and possibly triggering. Sometimes, when people recall trauma or when people remember experiences, what they're remembering is how situations affected them, and that's a reality. I am sharing my reality. There may be people who have knowledge of these situations and remember them differently, but my perception of these experiences is my truth. How I perceived these things had an impact that is unique to me, and it is imperative that I honor that impact as I relay these experiences to you. I hope that my willingness to share will empower you to honor your own lived experiences, regardless of other people's perceptions of those same occurrences.

Here

Life is not as tragic as we make it
Nor as happy as we paint it

Somewhere—between here and there
Lies life—raw and sensuous, fresh and demanding

In that life—I will immerse myself

July 2, 1993

1

....

WHO NEEDS NINE MONTHS?

My dad was a lot of things, but a milkman, he was not. I, however, and according to my family, was the milkman's daughter. If you've never heard that colloquialism before, it is reserved for children who don't look like their siblings and implies that those kids may have a different father. The original connotation is that the child's mother must have had an affair with the milkman. This was not literally the case in my family, but it was clear that I didn't fit in from the very beginning.

I was the youngest of three; my sister was older by ten years, and my brother was older by four. Mom was married three times; each marriage produced a child, and I was the only biological child of her third marriage to my father (I wouldn't discover any of that until much later). My sister, whose father was Cuban, is five feet three at best, with black curly hair and dark eyes. My brother is five feet ten inches tall with a Dominican father, dark, thick hair, and brown eyes. Now, picture my mother. She likes to describe herself as five feet one and three-quarters of an inch. In actuality, she's barely five feet tall, but she is five feet of beauty. In her youth, her hair was jet black, and she was of a darker complexion as well. She was petite but curvy with dark eyes, a picturesque Cuban woman. She had the style and carriage to match her form, always made up, always wearing heels, always perfumed, and always wearing jewelry. Based on my mother's and siblings' appearances, I understand why I was pegged as the milkman's daughter. I looked nothing like them. I am five feet nine inches tall now, but I was five feet seven by the fifth or sixth grade. My hair was really light when I was younger, and I have bright blue-green eyes, features that I got from my Brazilian father. My siblings both had very typical Latino features, and I did not. Furthermore, if you saw a family picture of us when I was a child, the milkman's daughter references would make perfect sense to you, too.

The physical differences weren't the only factors adding to the milkman's daughter theory in my family dynamic. In addition to the obvious physical differences between my siblings and me was a seemingly ever-widening gap between our personalities. My sister and I, for example, are like night and day. She was very much into everything girly and traditionally feminine. Pink, dresses, ruffles, and dolls held her interest, while my mind was far from all of that. Not to mention the fact that there's a ten-year age gap between the two of us, which was a constant reminder of our dissimilarity. Add in the fact that we shared a bedroom (and a bed for a long time) until I was seventeen, and you can see how there may have been some tension there. Because she was the oldest, she got the final say about everything in the room. It was just my luck that we grew up during a time when rainbows were a huge deal among kids, so my sister once chose to decorate our room with rainbows and ruffles everywhere. As a tomboy, there was nothing that I wanted less than a bunch of rainbows, ruffles, and dolls, but because I was the youngest, my opinion didn't hold that much weight. I just had to live with it. Another difference we had to contend with was my inquisitive, somewhat rebellious, and extroverted nature versus her more introverted and demure nature. I wanted to run around barefoot, be dirty, and get into adventures in nature, while my sister wanted to curl her hair, do nails, and wear Gold LeMay. We were just oil and water who happened to share genes and a bedroom, but little to nothing else.

Then there was my brother. The closeness that I lacked with my sister seemed as if it could be compensated for with my brother, since I projected more of what was thought to be masculine tendencies back then.

I was, after all, a self-proclaimed tomboy. I remember only having one Barbie; it was the weird one that kissed. She had a button on her back that, when pushed, would make Barbie arch her back and push her head forward for a kiss. It even made a little kissing noise. I thought it was so weird, but I would still play with it, not to make her kiss any Ken dolls, though. I would just put her into my brother's Tonka trucks, and I would make her fit in with his G.I. Joes, just like I was determined to fit in with my brother. I had more fun playing with him and tried my best to be like him, probably more to his chagrin than anything. I'm sure he saw me as this annoying little sister who just wanted to tag along with him all the time. We got along fairly well when I was younger because I just did whatever he wanted to do. However, as we got older, and he began to be interested in dating, our bond began to weaken. I could tell I was becoming more of an annoyance than anything, and after a while, we found ourselves farther and farther apart.

When it came to the relationships with my brother and sister, the pieces just never did fit. I was always caught in this weird space of not really getting along with my sister. It was almost as if she was trying to be a mother instead of a sister, which I obviously rejected. My brother's and my relationship proved to be no less problematic. Trying to bond with him by attempting to be the little brother he never wanted did not work. Both of these relationships always left me feeling out of place, so the milkman's daughter idea felt very real. I knew we were related, but the bonds between us weren't strong enough to quell the speculation. It was clear that there was something different about me.

To add more context to this idea of not belonging in my family, we also need to consider the origins of my name and the circumstances surrounding my birth. During the 1970s, there was a popular Mexican telenovela called *Yesenia*. The main character, my namesake, is a light-eyed woman living amidst the romany dark-haired, darker-skinned gypsies. The actress playing the role is the famous Mexican blonde actress Fanny Cano. Coincidentally, this is the show that my mother had been obsessively watching during her pregnancy. The title character, and name of the show, is a spirited gypsy girl who falls in love with someone outside of the gypsy community—only to find out that she is not a member of her family at all—but a surrendered infant to the caravan. Who would have known that, like the show's protagonist, I would also be seen as an outlier in my own family?

In addition to that, everything about my birth story has always been framed as unusual and inconvenient by my family. Let's set the scene. In Hispanic Catholic households, communion is a big deal. Children would participate in Catechism, Bible study when they were younger, and back then, around the age of ten, they were expected to accept the Holy Communion for the first time. It signified that they are officially accepting a role in the Catholic Church. It's similar to the concept of the age of accountability in Christianity. The kids do all the things. They learn the little prayers, the Hail Mary, Our Father, etc. The girls get all dressed in white, and the boys are wearing tuxedos. They get their first rosaries and Bibles. It's a big deal!

On this particular day, which later became my birthday, my sister was preparing for her first communion. This was her moment. She had her mantilla, which is the veil that covers her head. My mom made her dress. She had a rosary, her little white gloves, and she was super excited. There's a party that had been planned for months and took a week to prepare the house, which was now full of guests. Mom had been dangerously busy up until this point. The week before consisted of my mom cleaning the house from top to bottom to prepare for the post-communion party. She had also spent most of the weekend cooking all the food for the party. Once everyone got back to the house after communion, my mother would serve as hostess for the party, and my sister would serve as star of the show.

At around four o'clock that afternoon, everybody was at the house after communion, and the party was in full swing, when all of a sudden, my mom, who was seven months pregnant at the time, started to feel bad. She was having contractions, probably a result of overworking herself in preparation for this party. Whatever the case was, her pretending that she was ok was not convincing anyone, and she was rushed to the hospital. Years later, when my sister would retell this story, she would declare that her life was ruined because both my parents had to leave for the hospital, while my sister and other family members had to stay back with the few guests who didn't leave. To this day, my sister is still so dramatic when telling this story. As my mom was being admitted into the hospital, she was vehemently telling the nurses, "This baby is ready. She is here!" The nurses replied that "she" (I) would have to wait, to which my mom fired back, "She's not waiting!" With that, I, Yesenia Braga, was born at 5:44 PM in the hallway at Resurrection Hospital in Chicago, Illinois.

Though I was admittedly my mom's easiest delivery, I also seemed to be the most inconveniently timed birth. For the next several years, I would constantly be told how I couldn't even wait to be born or how I ruined my sister's day by being born. It never got old to tell me that I had no eyelashes, only nail beds, no real fingernails, and that I hadn't really finished "cooking"—that I looked like a long skinny lizard as compared to my nine-pound and ten-pound siblings, I was only seven pounds at birth. Most of the stories of my birth are framed in a negative light. Add that to the constant reminders of how I must be the milkman's daughter because I don't look like my siblings, and you get a child who has to grow up with a constant sense of isolation and loneliness. That is not the lens through which a child should view her origin story.

On top of being named after the not-so-gypsy-looking telenovela protagonist, Yesenia, the other part of my name that added to the oddness I felt in my family is the fact that I don't have a middle name. In Hispanic and Latino culture, middle names are a defining part of one's identity. It's not uncommon for some Hispanic or Latino people to have four or five names. There is a great deal of significance tied to some of those names. Naming can have religious significance with people being named after saints, or children can be named according to historical traditions or after a relative. Then there's also the practice of marking family lineage, with individuals carrying both their father's and mother's last names to signify the family history or social status. I was just Yesenia. There was no Maria, no "de la" whatever. Just Yesenia Braga. Because I didn't have one, I now just use my maiden name as a middle name. Can you imagine how insignificant even the absence of a middle name felt when others in my family had one? It just seemed like another weird thing about me that made me unlike the rest of my family. An even more bizarre reality concerning my name is that I've recently discovered that "Braga," the surname I grew up identifying with my entire life, is not my real name. I don't know all of the details surrounding this most recent revelation, but I have it on good authority from Braga family members that my true heritage lies in a different last name; it's Araujo. I'm not surprised, though. My identity has been a constant topic of question and concern for me in my family for years. I am anxious to do the research in finding my true familial heritage and welcome the potential for new self-reflection and discovery that accompanies that journey.

Having to hear about my birth story in such a negative light on so many occasions definitely had an impact on me. I was indeed premature, arriving two months earlier than scheduled. However, there was a better way to frame that fact than focusing on the perceived slight inconveniences of my birth. We can start with the reality that my birth and life actually saved my mother's life. My mother was showing signs of pre-leukemia before she had me. Pre-leukemia is the old name for what is now known as Myelodysplastic Syndrome (MDS). MDS occurs when blood cells found in bone marrow start malfunctioning. Symptoms can include fatigue, unexplained bruising, frequent, easy bleeding, infections, bone pain, and a host of other ailments. Mom was never formally diagnosed with this disease, but it was clear that she was extremely sick. I look back at pictures of her right before I was born, and it's obvious that she's not well. Her skin looked discolored, and she looked underweight. We didn't know it then, but over the years, science has proven that pregnancy can often improve and even reverse the effects of some illnesses in the mother, which was the case with my mom. She would even say, in passing at times, that I made her get better. Despite the sparse acknowledgments of the benefits her pregnancy with me had, she never seemed to make that the focus of the story when speaking about me and my birth. Wouldn't that have been a beautiful story if the default had been, "Look what you did for me. Look how you saved my life," instead of "Look how impatient you were," or "Look how weird you are. You couldn't be born on time like the rest of my children."

I was different. That was obvious, but my differences were unique and should have been praised and encouraged. Yes, my birth technically crashed my sister's communion celebration, but I like to think I came early because I wanted to join the party. In actuality, my premature birth was probably caused by the fact that my mother had overdone it with preparation for the communion festivities, unintentionally inducing labor. My family tended to describe me as impatient because I was early getting here. I see that as a positive that followed me throughout life. I did everything early, reading, learning to ride a bike, advancing in academics far quicker than my classmates, never waiting for permission from anyone to accomplish my goals. These are all great ways to frame my so-called prematurity. Finally, the irony about me being dubbed the milkman's daughter is that for years, my family perpetuated the implication that I didn't belong, when in actuality, I was the only one of the children who was actually biologically related to my father. I didn't find out until years later that each of my siblings has their own stories to tell regarding the proverbial milkman. Not only was my dad not their biological father, but they also had different fathers from each other!

Birth stories are important. They shape the way children see themselves, at least for those formative years, and at most, for the rest of their lives. These stories are the very beginning of our origins, and what we think is funny, what we think is unique, or what we think is just a joke, critically affects children for the rest of their lives. Moreover, when we tell these birth stories or when we choose these names, we have to think about the child, not ourselves, not how we feel, but how that child will feel hearing it throughout his or her development. Some cultures believe so strongly in the significance of names that children don't get a name until well after they are born. In Ghanaian culture, a child is named based on gender, day of the week, and an older relative in hopes that the child will grow to one day, inherit the good characteristics of the ancestor for whom he or she was named. Indian culture commonly relies on the position of the stars when children are born to determine their names, and that position is usually linked to characteristics, divine beings, or life lessons. Serious thought and contemplation go into naming because those cultures understand how much that name will influence who that child becomes.

In a perfect world, that amount of thought and intention would go into the naming and origin story of every child. People, however, are flawed and imperfect, so some children have less than intentional naming processes and origin stories. Every single person deserves to be valued and told how important their entrance to and presence in this world is, but when that is not the case, I challenge people to rewrite their origin story for themselves. No one wants to feel like they were a mistake or an inconvenience, even if that might be the truth. We all want to find and embrace the significance of our entering this world. If you find that those charged with setting the atmosphere for your entry into the world and making sure you knew you were valued and loved when you got here, failed to do so, take ownership of that responsibility yourself.

Think about everything you've ever experienced or done. Then think about the person you want to become. What experiences or situations had to happen exactly as they did, exactly when they did, for you to be the person you are and become the person you want to be? Whatever those circumstances were, they had to happen just as they did, or you would've missed the occurrences that shaped you. No matter what has happened up until this point, or no matter what the story is that other people told you, you had to come on that day, in that hour, in that place. You had to go through that challenge or that victory for the rest of the dominoes to fall, to bring you to the moment that you are in today. The beautiful synchronicity of why you're born in the moment that you're born is so that everything else happens. If you just take that as your own, it means your origin is beautiful. When you think about it, recognize that those moments where you've been at the right place at the right time to help someone, to witness something beautiful, or to be a part of something magical would not happen unless everything before it happens. You rewrite your origin story by understanding your name and your journey is beautifully unique to you, despite how those in your life have framed it.

Though everybody indeed has the power to rewrite their origin story, we, as parents and guardians, the name-givers and narrators of the birth stories have to hold that responsibility as sacred. Too often, the narratives we tell are wrapped up in the funny, the absurd, or the emotions of the adults involved, and we don't tell the beautiful side of the birth. We're always so drawn into how long it took, how painful it was, who did this, or who did that. Children are hearing all of it, and they're attaching culpability to the negative. In Spanish culture, there is a phrase, "dar a luz," that, literally translated, means "to give light" and is used to describe giving birth. We should keep that in mind when speaking of children's birth. The experience should bring light, positivity, and beauty. I would hope that everyone who ever is part of a birth, gives birth, supports birth or witnesses birth helps to promote positive birth stories for children to give them a bright start to their future. That's the lesson.

Fragility of the Human Soul

The human soul seems so fragile—yet its essence is of
the tightest weave
Every thread in the composition is made of steel
As the woven product takes shape, we are born

Our soul is the blanket of our mind and heart
Like a shield that feels and reacts
Our strength of character is the thread count

Our soul lies innocent and trusting
While words and actions permeate the boundaries
Time and experience slowly harden the weave

When we no longer feel, and think and act—we then
start to die
We cannot live without the dying
It is in this that we are then human

November 11, 1993

2

....

THE DAY DADDY BROKE IN TWO

The Ani-Yunwiya, or the indigenous people of the southeastern United States who Americans know as the Cherokee, have a well-known proverb about two wolves. It's a very practical story about the duality of human nature. Basically, a grandfather was talking to his grandson about life. The grandfather tells the grandson that there are two metaphorical wolves living inside every person. One is full of anger, envy, arrogance, fear, greed, and pretty much all of the negative emotions one can imagine. The other wolf is full of joy, love, empathy, hope, compassion, etc. These two wolves are constantly at war. The grandson asks his grandfather which wolf wins, and his grandfather simply replies, "whichever one you feed". That proverb attempts to explain the innate duality of human nature. None of us are good or bad, but we are a mixture of both; I witnessed that dichotomy at an early age, in my father.

With one hazel eye and one brown eye, Dad was handsome but not pretty. The hair on his head was brown, while the hair in his beard had a little hint of red in it. His nose, so much like mine, was crooked due to a deviated septum. He stood about five feet, ten inches, had a great smile, and knew what to do with it. Dad was charming, or "sharming" as he pronounced it. When people would ask his age, he would say something like, "I'm forty and still sharming." Then he'd flash that smile, and he had you! Early on in my life, he would ask me, "Who's the most handsome man you know?" and I would say, "You, Daddy!" Then he'd follow up with, "Who's the smartest man, you know?" As rehearsed, I would say, "You, Daddy!" We did this for years, and it seemed like this lighthearted special interaction with a father and his daughter, but his constant self-declarations of his charm, good looks, and intelligence may have stemmed from a place of insecurity. He seemed to always need the reassurance of his intelligence and value.

In addition to his desire to be the most charming and intelligent man in the room, my father was also one of those people who wanted to be a jack of all trades. Unfortunately, I don't think he ever became the master of anything, but he knew enough about everything to convince those around him that he was a master at whatever he was doing. He could pick a guitar enough for you to think he played, but didn't. He could speak several languages enough to order food and impress people, but he wasn't fluent in more than Portuguese, Spanish, and English, which is still more than most people. That wasn't enough for my dad, though, so he would throw in a French, Italian, or German word into conversation here and there to add to his allure. My grandmother and other immediate family also made a big deal of his unique eyes, golden-brown complexion, and sun-kissed hair when he was a baby—this only perpetuated my dad's ego as an adult.

To truly understand my dad and his need to present himself in the most impressive way possible, you have to understand the circumstances surrounding his upbringing. My grandmother, my dad's mother, was born in Brazil at the turn of the nineteenth century at a time when it wasn't uncommon to see girls being married in their teenage years. Family legend has it that Grandmother was around fifteen when she married her first husband, who died, making her a widow in her early twenties. My dad was a product of her second marriage and was one of nine children who lived. This marriage is the one that I spent the majority of my life thinking my last name, Braga, came from, only to find out in my adulthood, through a family reunion, that it was not the case—my family name was actually Araujo.

According to family history, my grandmother was once making a trip by boat from one side of Brazil to the other to live with her next husband. Accompanying her on this journey were three older children and a young baby, my father. The steerage situation was similar to that of the Titanic in that the poorest of passengers, which included Grandmother and her children, were housed on the lower decks. A wealthy woman from the upper decks noticed my grandmother with this handsome baby and assumed that this young woman must have been overwhelmed with trying to provide for all of these children. The woman sent word by a servant that she was interested in buying my dad. She basically said to my grandmother, "You're young, and you've got more than you can handle with all of these kids. Let's make a deal, and I'll take this one off your hands right now." My grandmother, according to the story, famously rejected the woman's offer because my dad was her favorite. She would never let him go. My dad held on to that story with pride for most of his life. He realized that had my grandmother accepted that lady's offer, he would've had a very different life, one that probably would've afforded him luxuries and privileges beyond his imagination; my dad found validation in this story. It proved that he was wanted, but it also made him feel cheated of a better life he deserved somehow. Some rich lady was so taken aback by his looks that she wanted to buy him. He reveled in that, and the validation from that story served as the backdrop to who he was.

Dad was also a bit of a philanderer. He loved the ladies, and the ladies loved him, so much so that early on in Brazil, he found himself entangled with another man's wife, even though my dad was also married and had three kids (that we know of). His mistress' husband happened to be a powerful man, and my dad ended up having to leave town quickly after this powerful husband became aware of said affair. Dad left his wife, kids, and everything he had ever known in Brazil and moved to Chicago. I don't know what led a man who had grown up in the tropical temperatures of Brazil to The Windy City, but that's where he met my mom. They eventually got married, and Dad shared his dream of becoming a physician with my mom. That sounds like a noble goal for a new American immigrant to have, right? Well, there was one problem. Dad didn't have a high school diploma. Immediately after sharing these dreams and his dilemma with my mom, she jumped into action.

To understand this next part of my story, you must know one thing about my mother. She was and has always been a visionary, and she wasn't going to let the absence of a high school diploma prevent my father from fulfilling his dream of becoming a physician. I'm not completely sure of the details, but I know enough to know that my mom encouraged my father to lie about not having a diploma. They were able to finagle my dad's way into medical school, with the right documentation and a sponsoring physician. Once he was accepted, we moved to Miami for him to complete his medical education. Mind you, my dad spoke broken English and Spanish, but he was an extremely intelligent man who studied all the time. It was that tenacity and dedication that pushed him to complete all of his required coursework in both English and Spanish. After completing all requirements, my dad passed all of his board exams and coursework and officially became licensed to practice medicine in Florida. The next step was to find somewhere to set up shop. My dad petitioned through a charity organization that our family was a member of in Miami—Lions Club International—to go to this little, rural town just outside of Gainesville, Florida, to be the town doctor. The town needed a new rural doctor. My dad and his sponsoring physician offered to practice medicine in this small city, so that's where we went.

I started elementary school in that little town, and all seemed to be going well. We were very poor at the beginning, but eventually, things started looking up. Before we knew it, we were able to afford a three-bedroom, two-bath house. Then my father built the clinic, and we got a pool. We were steadily on this financial ascension, and with it, I began to notice that good wolf living inside my father. The rural community in which we found ourselves had some very poor residents. When people didn't have the money to pay my dad, he would enact a barter system instead. We would constantly get gifts on our doorstep. One of those gifts was cheese.

Yes, cheese. For years, I thought my mom was crazy and was just buying huge blocks of cheese. We would constantly tell her, "Stop buying all this cheese! This is too much cheese!" She would just look at us funny and tell us to stop complaining. Looking back, I realized that my mom wasn't buying that cheese at all. People were getting cheese as a food subsidy from the government and using it to pay my dad for medical services.

He did that for years. He was constantly exhibiting this weird sort of duality of being not the best dad to his children or the best husband to his wife, while also being this benevolent, compassionate doctor to his patients. He would make house calls in these rural areas of extremely poor people or of elderly people who had been forgotten. My father would treat them and not charge them. He would set bones and help people get to the big city when they had a really serious issue, because they had no way of getting there, and they couldn't afford an ambulance. It was so odd for me to see him at home, sometimes drinking too much, being violent and saying hurtful things, but then go to work and treat people for free or in exchange for food. His practicing medicine seemed to keep the good wolf fed and the bad wolf at bay for most of the time. Unfortunately for all of us, the dynamic between those two wolves would soon change.

It happened during my fourth-grade year. I remember when it came to a head because I was the lead in the school play that year. I was chosen to play Cinderella. We had already performed the production in the famous nightly performance for the parents and community, and we also performed it at other schools. On that day, however, we were to perform the play in front of my whole school during an assembly. I was excited for this opportunity, so you can imagine my devastation when I found out that someone else would play Cinderella for my school performance because I had somewhere else to be that fateful day. Someone, somewhere, somehow found out that my father lied about his academic background. This mystery person hired a private investigator to go to Brazil to investigate my father's educational credentials. Once the investigator got to Brazil, there was no school to verify whether or not my dad had completed coursework because the school had burned down. Either way, the sleuth had enough evidence of fraud to bring my dad's credibility into question and reported my father, and as a result, Dad had to appear before the state medical board for a disciplinary hearing.

It was a Friday morning, and we were headed to Marco Island, a resort community. I'm not sure why a state medical board would be meeting at a resort, but they were. When we arrived, the board seemed more interested in making their tee time than hearing cases. The process was quick. As my family waited for my father's trial, we watched, case after case, as the board members callously struck the gavels, changing people's lives forever. When it was our turn, we sat in the front row before the board. My dad was armed with a petition from hundreds of patients and several who were ready to testify on his behalf in person. The board didn't hear them, though. It was clear that those men couldn't care less about this Brazilian Latino who could barely speak English from some rural backwater town. They didn't even know who he was and didn't call one witness. They were completely disinterested. They just kept looking at their watches, as if this whole thing was merely an inconvenience holding up their golf games. I remember them saying a few words and hitting the gavel. My mother and sister burst into tears, while my father just stared blankly at the floor. All of his supporters and witnesses began shouting in protest, and I heard someone say, almost forebodingly, "It's all over."

It took me a while to realize that my father's license was revoked that day, and he could never practice medicine again. I could still hear that person saying, "It's all over." It was all over for him, in many ways. When we finally got home the next day, my father took a seat on the back porch, lit one of his famous cigars, and didn't say a word to anyone, not even me, for maybe forty-eight hours. My dad and I had a unique relationship. It had been evident from the moment I got home from the hospital. There are pictures of me sleeping on his chest as a newborn. I had difficulty sleeping as a baby, but for some reason, I would sleep fine on my dad's chest. Once I started growing up, I became his shadow. Wherever he went, I went, and whatever he did, I would try to do. Dad got a kick out of the fact that I would parrot whatever he taught me, so before I started kindergarten, he had taught me to name at least 200 bones in the human body in two languages. I was, basically, his little mini-me. I felt like he and I had a different connection than he did with my siblings. It was definitely something special, so my inability to get him to talk to me after the trial was a huge cause for concern. My dad loved being a doctor, so I imagine he thought to himself, *If I can never practice medicine again, then I'm not a whole person.* I watched him for two days, sitting in that chair, looking at the woods, and I saw transfiguration over his face. That was the day my daddy broke in two—the bad wolf started rising.

I had to go back to school the next Monday, which was an extremely awkward experience. Everyone knew what happened, so people were whispering about me behind my back. Teachers were looking at me with sorrow and sympathy in their eyes, and I didn't really understand what was happening, other than the fact that my daddy was broken. People brought gifts to the house and wanted to see him, but he wasn't the same. You could almost see that the light behind his eyes had dimmed. I tried to talk to him, but he was non-responsive. That was also the beginning of the end of my parents' marriage. He and my mom were never able to communicate effectively again after that.

Since Dad could no longer legally practice medicine, he became the clinic's administrator and hired another physician to actually treat the patients. He later bought a small, rural hospital and became the administrator there. However, that position proved to be challenging for him. He was too close to it, so he just became more and more frustrated. He was frustrated with the doctors, frustrated with the system, frustrated with insurance, frustrated with everything, and he was justified in his feelings. Healthcare was headed in the wrong direction. Insurance was becoming unaffordable for the average patient, and, though he couldn't practice anymore, that good wolf was still very much alive in him. My father was still advocating for the patients, from the costs of services to the quality of food served. He was one of the only people who would charge very little for a basic X-ray. Dad was constantly fighting the healthcare system on charges to the patients and the basic costs of running a hospital. The good wolf was fighting for a more affordable healthcare system, while the bad wolf in his personal life was hiding affairs and alienating his children. He spent less time with us, as if facing us was just too hard. He was both a champion of the people, professionally, and an emotionally absent father and husband. Those two wolves still existed in my dad, but losing his license gave him less reason to feed the good wolf. Eventually, the bad wolf took over, and my dad was never the same. We never regained our special father-daughter closeness.

Watching all of this unfold had a profound impact on me in several ways. Seeing my dad break was heart-wrenching. This was someone whom I idolized. To add insult to injury, I could now tell that the disappointment my mother had in him, she had now passed on to me because I was a product of him. If I was the oddball before, I was even more of an oddball after all of that. There is a poignant reminder of my mother's conscious or subconscious unequal affection for me that sticks out in my memory to this day. She used to have this bracelet with a huge medallion, the kind that Hispanic women favor. On one side, there's a profile of a little girl, and my sister's name is inscribed alongside it. On the other side, there's a profile of a little boy with my brother's name as the inscription. My mother never added a medallion to that bracelet with my name and profile. What kind of effect do you think that would have on a child? I brought it up to her once; she apologized, but she never remedied it. She said I was thinking too much into it, but how could I not? It would have been simple just to add another medallion to it. She never did.

I suspect that my mom's unwillingness to add a medallion for me to her bracelet may have been evidence of the resentment for my father, which is her healing battle to fight. I can't do anything about that, and I have learned not to internalize it. However, I realize that all of this could have been avoided if they had just started with the truth. That is the first of many lessons I learned after looking back at this time in our lives. As the old saying goes, "Everything that goes on in the dark must come to light." I saw what those dark secrets did to my dad. By the time he lost his license, he was so weighed down with secrets and lies that that one truth broke him. In addition to holding secrets about falsified educational credentials, he was holding the secret of not being my siblings' father, the secrets of his other family in Brazil, the secrets of infidelity in his marriage with my mother, and who knows what else. He had built this persona, this facade of a perfect life and family that was all standing on a fragile lie, a lie that shattered as soon as one tidbit of truth crashed into it.

Watching the consequences of that lie left such an imprint on me that I vowed to never recreate that scenario with my own life and family. I subconsciously made a vow to never hold secrets in my family, and I have kept that vow to this day. I don't hide things from my kids. We always have family meetings over the important stuff, and we head off any misunderstandings before they get bigger. I never wanted my kids to feel like my younger self. I was only a fourth-grader, but if I had enough mental capacity to memorize those lines for the school play, then I had the capacity to understand what was going on with my father. How I wish someone had taken the time to consider my feelings. All I needed was for someone to break the situation down in a way that I could digest, instead of just avoiding the conversation. Children can sense when things are wrong, and we owe it to them to try and make sense of impactful events concerning family, society, and the world at large.

Someone, preferably from my family, should have stepped in and talked to me. That would have made a world of difference at the time. The same is true for my father. He needed help when he was breaking, but no one was there. I guess everyone just figured he would be ok; he would figure it out. He didn't, though. I imagine he felt as alone as ever in those moments. I hate to think of what his life, all of our lives, could have been if he just had a listening ear and some way to process that loss in a healthy way. Fortunately, his pain was not all in vain. Living through the destruction that this lie inflicted upon my family probably prevented my children and other loved ones from facing the same kind of trauma I experienced. I learned to feed the good wolf in my own life, so that my children would never have to live with the pieces of a mother who had been broken in two. That's the lesson.

Reflection

The passions of man baffle even God
We feel where there is no life
We cry where there is no sorrow

Time can weaken, but not erode memories
We stand now, as before
On the edge of vulnerability
The wind brings new ideas—but whispers old thoughts

In the burial ground of our minds
We pay tribute to things which cannot speak

Date unknown

3

....

RELIGION, WORK AND DISBELIEF

I t's dark. The only light illuminating the room is from several candles lit to honor the presence of our spiritual guides. The room is sticky with the humidity of a summer night and bodies too close together in a space too small for comfort. I can barely smell the hint of Mad Dog 20/20 and the unmistakable citrusy fragrance of Florida water. I don't know how long we've been here, but my seven-year-old body and attention span are bursting with anticipation for the end of this session. I peek one eye open to see how close my mother is to wrapping this thing up, when finally she says, "Our guides have spoken. Yesi is in danger. She will be in an accident and die." The other voices in the room, my father, siblings, and a few members of our tight circle, let out an audible gasp. *What?!* I thought. *Did she just say I'm going to die? I'm only seven. How can this be?* Well, I obviously didn't die, but I did spend the next several days tied to my dad's belt with a dog leash to keep me safe from any hurt or harm until the danger prophesied by the spirit guides through my mom had passed.

The aforementioned experience recounts a typical night of Santeria-like practice in my family. Santeria (and its variations) is a religion that combines elements of Catholicism with the Yoruba religion of West Africa. To try and understand the origins and history of Santeria, one must look at the history of Cuba. The interesting thing about Cuba is though it was colonized by Spaniards, a majority of the population is comprised of people of African descent as a result of the Trans-Atlantic Slave Trade. The indigenous population of Taino people was decimated by disease, slavery, and the brutality of the Spanish colonizers, so eventually, the enslaved Africans and their offspring outnumbered both the Taino and Spanish people. What was left was this interesting, non-indigenous culture of a Caribbean island that is now classified as Afro-Cuban. Santeria is the brainchild of that Afro-Cuban culture. It is similar to other religions of African origins like Haitian Voodoo, Brazilian Candomblé, and Arará. The trademark of the religion is that it recognizes Roman Catholic symbolism, ideologies, saints, etc. and assigns them to images and deities associated with African spirituality. This religion is a unique representation of how cultures collided and how an oppressed group of people transformed the religion of their oppressors into something in which they could believe and from which they could draw strength.

My family practiced both their version of Santeria and Catholicism, and like most practitioners of Santeria, we practiced at home, for us in a small building behind our house called a *cuartito*, which is Spanish for "little room". To the naked eye, it looked like a pool house, or a glorified she-shed. The average passer-by would have never guessed that inside it was our own little church of Santeria. Now, there are many standard rituals and customs associated with Santeria, but as with any religion, people of different regions practice in ways that are specific to the local community of believers. We had our own version of Santeria. We took a little bit of traditions and exercises from a few different religions and spiritual practices. We incorporated candles, knot-tying, Florida Water, and rose water. There was no animal sacrifice or anything close to that, but every now and then, you might find us throwing some flowers at an intersection or consulting a medium. It was a hodgepodge of different practices that we melded together to fit our spiritual taste. My parents believed heavily in the spiritual connection with the dead and the spirits that Santeria promoted. They referred to our sessions as "work" and took our commitment to working very seriously. Whenever it was time, at least one night a week, one of them would say, "Oh, we have to work tonight, so you're not going to watch TV. You're not going to go out. You're not going to do anything. We're going to work tonight." We all knew that meant meet at the pool house, so we would put it in our calendars: " Work tonight."

I don't have any proof that our religion was legitimate, and I don't know if I fully believed in anything they told us or anything we did. Surprisingly enough, though, I didn't fully disbelieve it either. My mom, however, was fully invested. She fancies herself a medium, which is a person with the spiritual ability to contact and communicate with spirits. Mom was the conduit through which we connected or spoke to all of the beings around us. From a fairly early age, I was expected to sit still through these rituals of rope-tying, silk-tying, flowers, mixtures, symbols, chalk drawings, and lots of meditation. I was expected to believe without a doubt and without any proof. Even if I didn't fully understand what was going on, the adults would say, "¡Concéntrate!" which means "concentrate" in Spanish. How was I supposed to concentrate? I was a child! The last thing on my mind was meditating on spirits and talking to dead people. In fact, my favorite activity while working was to close my eyes when they said so and then, immediately open one eye to see what everybody else was doing. The more they would urge me to concentrate, the more I would silently rebel and sing a song in my head or simply think of anything other than what was going on around me. Mind you, I had always been told that our spirit guides could see us and were watching at all times, but somehow they never saw me with my eyes open. If they did, they never told my mom or anybody else that my eyes weren't closed during these sacred times of meditation and concentration.

This work we were doing seemed so futile. I can remember many times just watching everything that was going on and thinking to myself, *This is an incredible waste of energy and space* because we were always asking for something–goods, riches, wishes. Whatever the request, it always seemed out of reach of the people. Santeria and Catholicism had that in common. Just as I sat with one eye open and one eye closed in that little house in the back of my house at least once a week, for at least thirty minutes to an hour, meditating and trying to contact dead spirits, my parents also ensured that we were up early for Mass on Sunday morning. My mother was raised Roman Catholic, so she made sure we went to catechism, basically, classes that taught about the core beliefs of Catholicism, and church every Sunday morning. Even after watching and participating in baptisms, communion, and other seemingly important rituals, parishioners of both these religions never seemed to get what they wanted while here on earth. There was always this promise of things getting better, either one day in the future or after we die. I recognized this early on in my childhood and wondered, *Why not today?* The idea of practicing these religions faithfully and without flexibility, just not to be able to enjoy the fruit of your labor until after death felt exhausting to me. I couldn't wrap my tiny brain around why the people didn't just cut out all the religious parts of their spiritual beliefs and just do what it was that they were praying or hoping for. If you want a good life, love people, and do good. If you want peace, stop fighting. Why don't we just live in gratitude because life's pretty good right now? It seemed so simple to me. Why did we need to go to church or work to have someone else tell us how to do that?

The night I was tied to my dad because of a warning from the guides showed me how easily religion was used to control people. After getting word from the guides that I was in immediate danger, I was literally attached to my dad's belt loop by a dog leash. That night, I slept in my parents' room on a little mattress, which was fine. I liked sleeping on the floor next to my dad. I put my hand up, and he threw his hand down to hold mine. I liked that part. I felt closer to him at that moment, but I wasn't old enough to realize how traumatic the next few days would be. We took a weekend and a few extra days off as a family and went to our little house on the Suwannee River. It wasn't anything grand, just a small hunting shack, but it was a getaway for my family, a place we could go and be one with nature. We would all pile into the back of my dad's pickup, which was still legal back then, and head there for the weekend. My mom would cook, and dad would hang out by the fire he built or shoot his rifle, while the rest of us just relaxed. It was long weekends of doing nothing, where I would just walk the shoreline of the Suwannee for hours at a time.

This particular trip was different, though. I was tied to my dad the entire time. Everywhere he went, I went. I remember having to go to the bathroom. Dad says, "Okay," so we went into the bathroom. He turned his back, and I used the restroom. During these days of being tied to my dad, I was reminded that the spirits were watching me and that I was going to die. I spent that time completely paranoid and on edge, waiting for tragedy to strike. After about four or five days of nothing happening, my parents decided that the danger was over, and I was released from my dad's leash. Apparently, since I was watched over carefully, we had avoided my death. Nobody questioned whether the warning was actually real. Was it really about me, or was it maybe about controlling my philandering dad for a few days? We just resigned to the fact that listening to the prophecy saved my life. This incident made an indelible mark on my perception of religion and the harm it can cause. Think of what that kind of control and manipulation can do to a young, impressionable mind. I'm still working to get over the trauma from that experience now. It was wrong, and the whole experience just increased my growing skepticism for organized religion.

As time passed, I began to observe more and more the similarities and differences between Santeria, Catholicism, and other religious denominations. I began asking permission from my parents to go to church with friends. They would agree. I'm sure they saw my desire to attend church as a positive endeavor. However, my motivation for visiting other churches was more out of curiosity and observation than any pious pursuit that my parents may have believed. We still lived in North Florida, so the diversity of religion wasn't booming, but I was able to visit congregations of Christianity–Methodist, Baptist, etc. One particular church that sticks out in my memory had a pew just for kids that they called the "ant bed" because kids always had "ants in their pants." They just couldn't sit still for longer than a few minutes. While sitting there with the other "ants," I had the same thoughts I had while sitting through "work" with my family. I noticed that all these religions or denominations were basically the same. They all claim to be privy to some universal truths that they disseminate to their followers either through some sacred text or oral tradition. They all have their rituals, symbols, songs, and traditions, and at the end of the day, they all want their followers to obey their rules and come back the next week.

With Catholicism, there were the teachings of the beliefs and the testing that followed to make sure believers could articulate what their doctrine was. Santeria didn't have any formal tests, but believers still had to prove their belief through different means, like wearing white for a certain amount of time. All of it seemed like control, especially when it came to the women. Even as a child, I found it interesting that at least within the Catholic Church, there weren't a lot of women in positions of leadership or public-facing roles. It was all men and altar boys. All the nuns could do was be married to Christ and cover themselves. They were always behind the scenes, doing all the work. There were women there, but the men were the ones in charge. Though some women had certain elevated positions, their power was still dependent on what the men had to say. The women who actually did taste some semblance of power or authority were only seen as such based on their connection to motherhood or purity. You were pious and deserving of elevation, only if you were seen as a pure mother or a pure virgin. That bothered me. My overall sentiment about religion was that I just didn't get it. I couldn't figure out what all the hubbub was about, and I definitely couldn't figure out why some people let religion divide them. We were all doing the same things, just with different names, and it always seemed to lead back to control. Believe in this, or something bad will happen to you. Pray, hope, and strive to live like this, and you'll see paradise in the afterlife. No matter whether it was Santeria, Catholicism, or anything else, the followers were being told what to believe and how to feel, and that's where my thoughts about belief diverged from what was being shown to me.

I was still only a child when I started coming to these conclusions about religion, and we didn't have the kind of family dynamic that allowed me to just stop going to church. I just chose my own silent rebellion. I still had to go to work, but while I was there, being admonished to concentrate and meditate, I would just sit there, hold hands, and pout. The whole time, I looked like I was on the same page with everyone else, but I'm really thinking, *Nope; I'm not thinking about this. I'm not going to do this.* I wanted to play. I didn't want to participate in this, and I didn't want to wait until some treasure fell into our family's lap or some big fortune came that would take all our problems away. From what I could see, we were good. We ate every day. We were safe, and we slept soundly every night. What else did we need?

For the rest of my childhood, it was that silent rebellion that kept me from complete disillusionment regarding religion. I still went to church and work, but I made sure to be in charge of my own thoughts and feelings regarding faith and the supernatural. These beliefs are what now guide me in my adulthood. I still believe in the existence of something beyond us. I believe in nature and the energy around us. I believe I've had encounters with the supernatural, but I haven't had those encounters through any ritual, religion, or anything that's been manifested by someone else. I've seen things on my own. I've experienced things on my own, but I haven't caused or ritualized them. They've just been echoes, residual traces of spiritual energy that I've felt just by being open. There were no rituals or work that I went through to connect with the energy around me. That is just such an incredible waste of time and energy, but again, I always think those rituals are just a manipulation of people. We buy the candles, the ritual kits, and we pay other people to tell us how to do it. It just becomes another sort of machination of man that we need someone else to guide us to be ourselves, which I don't think is necessary. We can just step outside into the forest, out into nature. The energy is there. The connection is there. Science has shown us that when a tree is cut down, the surrounding trees actually send nutrients to the roots of the stump. That's community! That's nature showing us how we should show up for one another when we're in need. That's nature showing us that we're all connected and that one person's pain affects their entire village.

Outside of my realization that my closest connection to religion and belief has been my connection with nature, I've also come to understand a few more lessons about religion and belief. First, belief is important, but I don't think anyone should be told how to believe or what to believe. People should not be controlled by religion. People should follow whatever faith or belief that makes them happy. That's it. Belief can be a good thing or a crushing thing. Anytime it's crushing you, that's not belief. That's control. Everybody needs to find their belief system and hold on to that. Next, belief shouldn't be hard. We shouldn't have to go through all these classes and tests or perform rituals or rites to access spirituality. We don't need rules to believe. You either believe, or you don't. Religion shouldn't be "work". Belief just is. That's the lesson.

Can you hear joy?

Hear it echo through the trees
Angel-like maidens feel that joy
It causes the heat in their cheeks
It brings the girl to the boy

Hear it echo through the trees
The uncontrollable laughter starts ringing
Throughout the halls and rooms
That same joy starts the singing

Hear it echo through the trees
As man seizes the hand of nature
Very assured that their symphony
Has a life in the future

Hear it echo through the trees
That soft and silky tune
It keeps playing on and on
As unconditional as the moon

Hear it echo through the trees
That sound that saves our souls
That one sound that lifts us
And saves us from life's tolls

Hear it echo through the trees
That sound is joy, that sound is God
It whips throughout this world
Like a stallion on earth—it will trod.

December 2, 1988

4

....

TAKE A WALK IN MY WOODS

Recently, I stumbled upon a term that I thought was really funny–forest bathing. When I heard it, I laughed because I imagined a person standing in the middle of the forest rubbing leaves and branches all over themselves. That mental picture was humorous until I did some research. It turns out that I have been forest bathing since I was a child, and no, it does not involve rubbing one's body with leaves. That just sounds like a recipe for a rash. Forest bathing is a term derived from the Japanese word "shinrin-yoku," which, loosely translated, means to "take in the atmosphere". The Japanese started this practice in the eighties as a remedy for burnout for its tech employees and to encourage its citizens to appreciate and protect their forests. The benefits were immediately evident, as research has proven that spending time in nature is good for one's health. This concept is not new, however. For millennia, people have looked to nature for healing and relaxation. Forest bathing just put a name on that practice.

There is no real, formal method to forest bathing. One can practice, simply, by taking a walk and intentionally focusing on the sights, sounds, smells, and feelings of the surrounding atmosphere. There is also the possibility to hire guides to facilitate structured meditations for a more tailored experience, but really, all you need to do is go outside and be present. It doesn't even have to be a forest. It could be a rainforest. It could be a jungle. It could be an island, so that would be island bathing. The whole point is, you're in nature away from all man-made items.

Let's take a moment to guide you through the experience. First, go outside. Find a place to sit or stand. Close your eyes for a few seconds, and when you open them again, spend time connecting and noticing everything around you. Notice the movement. Notice the animals. Notice the plants, the leaves, the trees. What do you smell? What do you see? What do you hear? Then, with your hands and, maybe, with your bare feet, it's time to feel. What does the ground feel like? Try to sit down or lie down. I don't like spiders, so I'm not lying down. Touch the leaves. Are they crinkly? Are they soft? Pick up a stick. Feel it. Smell it. Only if it's safe, taste it. Wherever you are, you're trying to immerse all of your senses in the natural world around you. That's forest bathing.

Forest bathing has unknowingly been a part of my life since childhood. In sixth grade, I had an assignment requiring me to write about my source of inspiration and safety. I wrote about being in the woods–in nature. As an adult, one of the things that I've been working on concerning my trauma, some of which I discuss in this book, is this hypervigilance of never feeling safe. All the traumatic experiences in my life created this lingering lack of safety, but the one place that I've always felt safe is when I'm completely immersed in nature. I knew that as a child. Nature felt more like home than my actual home. Whether I was consciously aware of it or just so connected to nature that I gravitated to it, I constantly found myself somewhere outside.

Fortunately or unfortunately, depending on perspective, my parents lost track of me all the time. We had a little cattle fence that ran around the backyard because there was a cattle farm behind us. I learned very early on to take a small ladder and throw it over the cattle fence. That created steps on the front of the fence and steps on the back. Then, I would encourage the dogs to jump over the fence. Sometimes I would just push them over the fence when they hesitated. Finally, I would climb my little ladder, take the dogs, and away we would go for hours at a time! One of my favorite things to do while in the woods was climbing trees. I'd go out there with a book in my pocket. Then I would find a really good branch, climb up, and read for hours. Sometimes, I would get so comfortable that I would fall asleep up there. Whoever was supposed to be watching me should have been fired! Whether it was my older siblings or my parents, they rarely ever knew where I was. Looking back, those were really unsafe circumstances for me, roaming the woods of rural North Florida as a pre-pubescent girl, but ironically, those were the times when I felt the safest. I would be gone for hours, just me, the dogs, and the woods. I was doing just what that term forest bathing suggested. I was listening and looking at everything, from the tiniest bugs on the ground to the largest birds in the air, and because I don't like spiders, I was watching for them, being very clear of where they were. I noticed everything, and somehow that process brought me joy, peace, security, and healing all at the same time.

Due to my ongoing internal conflict with religion as a child, nature subconsciously became my place of worship. The more time I spent there, the more I began to wonder at all the marvels of the earth. I would look at my surroundings and think about how awesome it was and how every-thing was working together. I thought to myself, *There is energy all around me right here. This is something to believe in.* I could see the world turning, the earth doing its thing, and thought, *This is beautiful.* I remember, even as a small child, thinking, *This is what we should be doing, protecting this, working with this, living within this community.* These thoughts brought me to the conclusion that my belief system, my religion, was nature. Walking in the woods became my belief system. When I needed to find peace, find myself, or feel safe, I would escape into whatever natural environment was closest to me for however long I could, and it became my place of refuge.

It wasn't just being present in nature that provided me with the peace and comfort that I needed to fight the sometimes chaotic energy and atmosphere of my homelife, it was also the understanding of how nature works that brought me peace. I found purpose in knowing that it shouldn't be destroyed to make me comfortable. I became a protector of it. I recognized that we're supposed to be a part of it, but we weren't sup-posed to tear it down. We're not supposed to replace it. We are to admire it, appreciate it, but not try to impose our human needs or conveniences over it. Sometimes, we take the purity of nature for granted. We assume that just because this beautiful piece of land exists, we should build a house here. We walk through the woods, and instead of just observing the sounds and symphony of noises occurring naturally, we fill the space with our voices, with conversation or any other variation of noise. What nature has taught me through my years of communing with and observing it is that there is no need to add anything to it. We don't need to be louder, brighter, or bolder than nature, so I began to ask myself questions about our relationship with nature. How do we interact with it without imposing our importance over it? How do we observe, enjoy, and use nature as we need it, without depleting and destroying it? How do we find that balance? Those answers would start coming to me as I grew older.

My walks in nature followed me into adulthood, and the more I walked, the clearer the need for balance between people and nature became. I started referencing some of the belief systems of old civilizations, and I purposely refer to them as civilizations, because some of their practices and beliefs were deemed savage and uncivilized by their colonizers. The indigenous people of the Americas, for example, were constantly referred to as primitive or uncivilized because of the perceived simplicity of their culture and systems by the colonizers. Modern-day Americans, as descendants of those who colonized this land, believed their systems to be better and more civilized, and as a result, ended up destroying almost all of the civilizations of the native people. However, based on how civilizations like the indigenous people of America interacted in harmony with nature, I think they actually had it right. They were not uncivilized people. The first people of the Americas had many different methods for preserving and protecting the land that were largely ignored and grossly neglected by settlers when building America's towns and cities. Take the nomadic tribes, for example. They had enough knowledge and respect for nature to move when they recognized they were depleting the resources too quickly. As a result, they lived on this cycle of rest and use that preserved the soil for future use.

Indigenous people also used controlled burning techniques to rid areas of invasive plants, control overpopulated animal groups, and prevent larger fires. That is the balance we need and the answer to some of the questions I posed earlier. These techniques not only showed the sophistication of the indigenous people's knowledge of nature, but it showed the respect and honor they had for the land on which they lived. It's part of the protection and preservation of nature that we need to promote and embrace more to make sure that our earth is well taken care of and available for all of us to enjoy for generations to come.

If you haven't noticed it yet, I'm passionate about nature and all of the benefits forest bathing can bring. I think many people can't fully appreciate nature because they have too much separation between inside and outside in their lives. In this sense, "inside" is anything that is man-made or involves man-made systems, while "outside" is anything relative to nature or naturally occurring phenomena. For some reason, many people want to keep things in their lives separate. There's a category or label for everything, in all areas of our lives–physical, mental, emotional, social, and professional. We have a tendency to do so much compartmentalization that we end up interrupting the natural energy flow of our lives. Humans forget that we are nature, too. We aren't man-made. We, too, are naturally occurring phenomena. When I would take my walks in the wilderness as a child, it almost felt like I was trying to be more like an animal and less like a person. What I didn't know then is that I was really just trying to belong somewhere, and I could feel that I belonged in nature because I do. We all do. We're not artificial substances. We're naturally occurring beings, and how beautiful is that? Our systems are amazing, naturally occurring systems. If we leave them alone, they will work. They will adapt and change as necessary and thrive without outside interaction. We still eat; we still poop. We still sleep. We can exist without the assistance of any of the technology, any of the things around us, so that means we belong. We're good. We're meant to be here, and if that's not religion, I don't know what is.

My walks in the woods showed me that I'm meant to be here. I'm enough, and all is well. That became my way to reconnect with a belief system that no one forced on me, that felt comfortable and wasn't crushing me. There was nobody there telling me how to do it; there were no books to read, no rules to memorize. I just had to be present and aware of my surroundings. I didn't have to wait to die to find peace. I didn't have to chase a brass ring to find peace. Just being there gave me peace, and that was important to me.

This connection to nature became my new religion. I didn't have a way to articulate the change at the time. All I knew was that it was positive, energizing, and flexible enough to grow and change as I grew, and grow, it did. When I was young and just discovering this safe space in nature, the idea was very singular and literal to me. I was searching for somewhere to belong, so the feelings I felt when in nature were a direct answer to the longing I had for a home that I didn't have at my actual address and with my biological family. As I've grown and traveled, however, I have been able to connect with nature in many ways all over the world. I have been to every continent except for Antarctica and Africa. I've experienced forest bathing in actual forests, but also in the mountains and next to rivers. I have been in nature in all of these countries all over the world and have found that same oneness all over the world that I also found in the woods surrounding my childhood home in rural North Florida.

One of the main commonalities we have as human beings is the desire to belong. For most people, though, that desire never broadens further than the narrow vision of connection to their immediate family or community, but for me, this religion of nature shows that I belong, not just to my little family or circle, but in this world. That discovery, that we belong in a bigger sense, is what I believe to be the real security that everyone is looking for. It's the grander sense of certainty that we're not alone, no matter where we go. Knowing we can travel to a completely different state, country, or continent and take a walk in the woods, sit by a stream, or hike up a mountain and still feel complete connection is the broader sense of community that every human being can access in nature if they are open enough to recognize it. Similarly, being able to walk or sit next to someone you don't know and exchange a glance or smile is the community that lives in all of us, regardless of how deeply it's buried under bias, prejudice, or ignorance. It's innately embedded in us, and the more we interact with people outside of our own little bubbles and spheres of influence, it will rise to the surface and happen naturally because that's how it works in nature.

That's the crux of the evolution that I've taken. I can have community with someone on the other side of the world without speaking the same language because I know I belong wherever I am. That's what I love so much about replacing religion with nature. There is no place in nature that's not accepting of me. I can't be excluded because I'm a part of nature simply by being born. One of the many problems with organized religion is this artificial need for one religion to be better than another, or for one religion to be the true religion. It's not that way in nature. If we look at nature and its connectivity, the way that a tree fits into its community is different from the way a dog fits into its community, which is also different from the way a fish fits into its community. Nobody is going to argue that the tree's way is better or worse than the dog's or the fish's. How they exist in nature is irrelevant. The connection is what's important. Everything that exists in a given ecosystem is there for a purpose and holds some level of importance to the well-being of the environment as a whole. In other words, everything belongs. That truth is the same for human beings as they exist in nature and community with each other. We all belong, and we all have a common energy of good living in us. It is our responsibility to embrace and nurture that energy rather than wasting time looking for and emphasizing our differences.

As an adult, I fully embrace the concept of forest bathing, but for me, it's more than just taking a walk in nature. I try to make sure I am in tune with nature in some way as much as possible. My house is full of plants, and I always make sure there is an animal in my life. When I'm home, I'm barefoot most of the time in order to actually feel the floor and stay grounded. Of course, I still take walks as much as possible, whether they are just around my yard or at a nearby park or trail. The same practices apply, though, no matter where I am. I have become so accustomed to this communion with nature that my body makes me aware of when I have been neglecting that relationship for too long. I feel discombobulated, rudderless, and like I need to get grounded. I start feeling like a battery that needs to be recharged. I even start to feel anxiety creeping up on me. When that happens, I have a visceral need to go make physical contact with the trees, grass, mud, or dirt, and so I do. I'll do something as simple as go outside in my backyard, take my shoes off, and just walk around in the grass. If need be, my husband and I will take a trip to the Florida Panhandle, sit on the beach, and let the smell of the salt water and the coolness of the ocean breeze just overtake us. In those times, I feel like I'm being cleansed, renewed, and reconnected.

Anytime I find myself forest bathing, I'm intentional about listening and observing how the creatures and environment interact with each other in their ecosystems. That intensifies the experience. I challenge you to do the same. The next time you're in the park or on a trail, take a moment to observe your surroundings. Sit down on one of the benches, or heaven forbid, sit on the ground. Take your shoes and socks off; put your feet in the grass, and then watch. Look down and into the grass. You'll see an entire universe in there–little ants, little bugs, and other little creatures. Watch what's happening; smell the air. Watch the movement, and feel the breeze. Do that for a short time, and the peace that comes over you, the energy release, will be a refreshing break from the hustle and bustle of everyday life. I'm not guaranteeing some orgasmic, out-of-body experience for you, but if you get still and allow your senses to take in the beauty that is Mother Nature, hopefully you will be able to experience that same feeling of belonging and security that I found as a child and hold dear as an adult. That's the lesson.

Many Ones

In the depths of my solitude
I find many friends
Warm, funny, strong, and giving

In myself, I find myself
I am my own friend
Understanding, comforting, and believing

Where once I felt alone
I now find comfort
There are so many of us
Deep inside of me

One for each occasion, one for each situation
If an outsider should ever join in—
It would be a warm homecoming
Why not welcome a new and different friend?

August 2, 1993

5
·········

LOVE AND DRUGS IN MIDDLE SCHOOL

The year is 1986. I'm a five-foot-seven-inch, gangly, awkward thirteen-year-old navigating one of the most tumultuous times in human growth and development–middle school. My middle school experience, for the most part, was probably like that of many other people. I had my share of insecurities, acne on my arms, identity crises, and the standard middle school crush. Think Elvis Presley as a thirteen-year-old. He didn't actually look like Elvis, but he had Elvis-like features. His smile–that was it. It was a sneaky, little, sinister smile, like he was up to something, which turned out to be true; nonetheless, there was something about that smile. I like people who know how to smile and have charismatic facial expressions that convey what they're thinking and feeling all over their faces. They don't have to have a pretty face. They just have to have an emotional face. My crush had one of those faces, and he was tall! I'm already naturally tall, but in middle school, when most boys hadn't yet gone through their growth spurt, I was like a tree towering over them. My crush was one of the few boys who was taller than I was. Needless to say, I was infatuated.

One day, while sitting in class, seemingly minding my business and watching my crush like a hawk, I noticed that he was acting squirrely. He couldn't sit still, and he seemed nervous. He had one of those athletic duffel bags that kids used to carry their gym clothes in between his chair and a classmate's. He seemed to be showing the other student something. I didn't know what he was saying, but I could tell that he was bragging and showing off. I looked down into his duffel bag, and it was stuffed with bricks of pot. It was full! As he zipped the bag closed, he noticed me looking. Mind you, this is somebody who'd never really given me the time of day. I had been crushing on him for at least four years, but he'd never even acknowledged me—this far from girly, tomboy who probably tried a little too much when in his presence. Now, all of a sudden, as if he had just discovered my existence, he smiled at me and said, "You didn't see anything."

I didn't know what to say. I just looked back at him, and he was really pouring it on. Looking back, I don't even know how he knew to do what he was doing, but he was doing that thing guys do when they know they're charming, when they know you're attracted to them. It felt like that common scene in every teen movie or rom-com you've ever seen where the female protagonist is actively daydreaming about the school heartthrob, and the lights go dim around everybody but him. He smiles, and a twinkle forms in his eye as he winks. That's what this guy did. Then, he winked and asked me, "You won't say anything, right?"

As I sat there, my heart must have broken into a million pieces. Here's my crush, the object of my affection, the only guy actually taller than me at the time, on whom I thought the sun rose and set, basically, asking me not to snitch on him for bringing a bag full of marijuana to our middle school! It was bad enough that he brought it to school, but based on his follow-up conversation with his friend, he was intending to sell it to kids in our grade and younger. I could slowly feel my attraction to him start to dissipate. Then I thought about the fact that the one time he showed any interest in me was because he was trying to avoid the very real possibility that I would tell on him. At that moment, I decided that I didn't care how cute I thought he was; I wasn't ok with that. I wasn't so infatuated that I couldn't see that he was trying to use my affection for him to manipulate me into keeping his secret. Well, it didn't work because I told. I first confided in a close friend, who agreed with me that what he was doing was wrong and that I should tell a teacher. That's just what I did. As a result, the authorities made the single largest drug bust in that school district's history at the time. The sad reality of the situation, worse than the fact that my crush intended on selling drugs to children, is the fact that some deranged adult was using him as a drug mule.

Authorities tried and failed to keep my identity as the whistleblower confidential, but the town was small. Word got around quickly, and soon, everyone knew it was me. Administration even thought that I might be in danger, so they called my parents and suggested that I be escorted to school as opposed to me walking, even though I lived right across the street from school. My parents didn't seem to expend too much worry or concern about this situation. In fact, I don't remember them ever discussing it with me. It was the main topic of discussion on every-one else's lips, though. I was all but shunned at school. I felt like Hester Prynne in *The Scarlet Letter*; only, instead of having an "A" for adulterer pinned on my shirt, I had a figurative "N" for nark! Middle school was already hard enough, so I definitely didn't need this cloud of judgement and ostracism following me around. Any semblance of a social life dis-integrated for me after that one decision to tell. I couldn't understand it. Nancy Reagan was on television every other day telling us to "Just say no," and DARE-ing (Drug Awareness Resistance Education) to keep kids off drugs was the newest popular anti-drug programming in all of the schools. I decided to do what we were being taught, yet I was the one being treated like the bad guy.

To add insult to injury, somehow my crush, the adolescent drug dealer, found out that I was the rat. A few weeks later, he called me. He got my phone number and called my house. That night sticks out vividly in my memory because it was the same night that Geraldo Rivera, one of America's most popular talk show hosts and television personalities, aired his now-infamous TV special, *The Mystery of Al Capone's Vaults*. If you're not familiar with this event, let me tell you, it was a big deal back then. There had been long-standing folklore around the notorious gang-ster, Al Capone's, vaults at the Lexington Hotel in Chicago. Capone ran his business from the hotel from 1928-1932. Because of Capone's criminal history and penchant for violence, he had secret tunnels and hidden rooms built into the hotel. Many people believed that he left money, valuables, or even human remains in the hotel for safekeeping from the authorities. That belief prompted Geraldo to take a camera crew, demolition men, and even the then Cook County Medical Examiner into the historical building in search of the remnants of Capone's past. Thirty million people tuned in to this special that night, including my mother, and thirty million people were left disappointed after two hours of viewing because there was nothing there.

The context of Geraldo's special is important to the events of my life that were happening at the same time as this historical television moment. While my mother was enthralled by the coverage of Capone, I was on the phone with my ex-crush. Yes, by this time, the infatuation had worn off completely. The first thing he said when we talked was: "Why did you do it? Why did you tell on me? You know it was none of your business." Then, as if to stick the knife in and turn it, he exclaimed, "I thought you liked me!" Keep in mind that I was barely thirteen when this was happening. I didn't quite have the emotional intelligence to pick up on manipulation and emotional gaslighting, but I guess my budding woman's intuition was ignited just enough for me to muster up the following reply, which went something like this:

"I think I just like the idea of you because I liked you up until I realized that you were willing to (By this time, I'd heard, through the rumor mill, that he was planning on setting up distribution to the elementary kids.) push drugs to kids younger than us! The fact that you were going to do that is so wrong and so gross that you got ugly, really fast! So, no! I don't like you anymore! You knew I liked you, and you've been ignoring me this whole time. You deciding to try to turn on the charm now to stay out of trouble shows that you're just an ugly boy."

After I explained to him that I no longer had an interest in him, he began to declare that my actions were a great example of why no one liked me. He stated that I was only just beginning to be pretty and catch boys' attention, but they would never try to date me after knowing I was the one who told on him. He also asserted that this was why no one ever invited me to their parties or desired to socialize with me. Now, I wish I could say that I was strong enough to stand up for myself in that moment and contradict his indictments of my social capital, but I wasn't. Even though I was no longer interested in him, his words still stung, and I thought my life might as well be over. At that moment, I needed to talk to someone who could help me work through that conversation and all of the previous events leading up to it. Unfortunately, I did not have that kind of support. I went to my mom and petitioned her to talk, to which she replied that she needed to see the end of Geraldo's special and that I needed to go wash dishes or something. When the program was over, she would have time to talk to me.

I couldn't wait until the special was over. It was a two-hour-long program. I was hurting, and I needed to talk to someone immediately! No one was available, and to me, that implied that no one cared. If no one cared, then there was no reason for me to be alive anymore, so–trigger warning–I went back in the kitchen as my mother instructed and proceeded to try and end my life. I took a steak knife and tried to slit my wrists. My family was in another room watching *Al Capone's Mystery Vaults,* while I was in the kitchen failing at suicide. Thankfully, I had no idea what I was doing and ignorantly picked the worst steak knife possible, so my attempt was unsuccessful. Then I felt stupid. I also felt a little bit like a failure because it looked so easy on TV and in movies. I couldn't even get that right.

Defeated, neglected, and just plain overwhelmed, I ran outside. I remember the night so clearly. It was late. I could hear Geraldo describing the scene in Capone's vault as I bolted out of the door, so it must have been almost eleven o'clock. I ran to the homemade tennis court that my parents had constructed in our yard. It didn't have a net, so I collapsed right in the middle of the court. I sprawled out like a starfish on the hard concrete and looked up at the sky. It was a clear night. I felt like I could see every star in the sky, and as I breathed in the night air, I began to sob my heart out. My animals must have felt my pain because soon, I felt every pet we had near me or touching me. The events of that night and the previous couple of weeks began to play like a movie reel in my mind. I was pretty sure I did the right thing. That boy was wrong. He should not have brought those drugs to school. It was wrong for him to even have them, let alone to try selling them to little kids. I knew in my heart that telling was important and responsible, so why did I feel so alone? Why did I feel guilty? Why had this person, whom I formerly perceived to be so cool, charming, and attractive, gone out of his way to embarrass and humiliate me when he knew he had done something wrong? Why weren't the people in my life coming to my rescue? How was Geraldo Rivera more important than me?

All of these questions floated around my head as I continued bawling my eyes out on that makeshift tennis court. Then, as if someone was slowly tightening a leaky faucet, my tears dried up. I looked up at the stars through blurry eyes, and I thought, *Well, it's not going to end here. When I go back to school, people are still going to whisper and avoid me, so what am I going to do about it?* I realized that if my own family didn't care to comfort and console me during this whole ordeal, then no one else was going to come rescue me. I had a decision to make. I could either sit there and feel sorry for myself, or I could be proud of myself. I decided to be proud. I did not just make the biggest mistake of my life. I was not crazy. He didn't get to sell drugs to little kids around me and buy my silence with his charm. No guy was worth jeopardizing my integrity in that way, especially not him.

I lay like that for hours that night, exhausted, but relieved. I was satisfied with myself and my decision, so I braced myself to return to school and face the continued ostracism. As expected, nothing had changed with the students. I never faced any outward bullying or taunting. There just seemed to be a collective agreement to ignore me. I still had a core group of friends, but most students just unanimously decided to make me an outcast. Even the teachers were acting strange. There was no school assembly to address what had happened or to warn the children of the dangers of drugs or how to speak out if they saw something. The adults at school, like my parents, acted as if nothing had happened. They went on with business as usual, except for one teacher. For the sake of anonymity, we'll call her Mrs. A. She was a black woman and a history teacher, which may be why she understood the social responses that occurred as a result of this drug bust. She saw the human condition through the patterns of our past and was a little more sensitive to how we respond as a collective. Anyway, when I got back to school, Mrs. A pulled me to the side, looked at me with that one eyebrow raised like only a strong, black woman can, and said very assuredly, "When you do the right thing, people won't always agree. Sometimes people are afraid to do the right thing. You did the right thing, and you should be proud of yourself. I'm proud of you." She gave me a big, old hug, and the little validation I had already permitted myself to feel just skyrocketed. Finally! I felt seen. Somebody else got it.

There are many different lessons I learned from this experience that I'd like to share with you. The first one I gleaned is how to handle being the object of someone's affections responsibly. People who are the recipients of love (whether authentic or not), infatuation, lust, or admiration, can expect a great deal of responsibility to accompany that affection, even if they don't accept the weight of that kind of influence. That responsibility is especially important if it occurs during a person's teen years because teens are so easily influenced and bruised. One can have a singular, bad conversation with one's crush that will leave remnants of embarrassment and low self-worth that may last a lifetime if the admirer doesn't immediately nip that in the bud with some self-healing exercises. One-sided admiration creates a power imbalance that has the potential to leave lasting trauma and damage on a young romantic.

How many times have we seen someone abuse that situation, power, or position for all the wrong reasons? Because I experienced this kind of manipulation with my seventh-grade crush, I was hyper aware of that power dynamic and was determined not to take advantage of it if I were ever on the other side of it. As life would have it, I was put in that situation later on in my adolescence. A friend of mine had a little crush on me and told me that he was the "Duckie to my Andie". If you don't get that reference, then you might be too young to have the core memory of watching *Pretty In Pink*. *Pretty in Pink* is a classic 80s teen romantic comedy in which Duckie is madly in love with his best friend and protagonist, Andie. In the end, Andie chooses the rich, hot guy instead of Duckie, so my friend telling me that I was his Andie was, basically, his way of telling me that he liked me, even though he knew the feelings weren't mutual. When he told me that, I immediately thought of thirteen-year-old me and how I felt about my crush. I smiled and hugged my friend dearly. Though I was honored that he thought of me that way, I was also clear that I didn't share those feelings. I thought he was an incredible friend and never once thought to belittle or disrespect him because the memory of that phone call in April of 1986 was still etched into my subconscious. It's a privilege to be admired by someone in that way. If you ever find yourself in a situation where someone holds affection for you that is not reciprocal, be careful with their emotions. It's ok not to return their affection, but it's never ok to take advantage of them or treat them poorly just because you can. Just remember, anybody can be a Duckie. What matters is how you treat him or her if you're an Andie.

Another lesson I learned from this concerns integrity and the importance of telling the truth. You've probably heard the common definition of integrity as the ability to do what's right even when no one is watching. Well, I believe that sentiment wholeheartedly. I would also add to that definition that integrity requires you to tell the truth even if people disagree with and distance themselves from you for doing so. This concept is especially relevant to the times we're living in now, in which it seems like facts don't matter. I want to formally oppose that trend, though. While it is easy to go with the flow, live in half-truths, and not speak up for facts, that just is not the right thing to do. Throughout my life, I have often stood up against disinformation and lies with the truth. People would often say that I was just "speaking my mind" or brand me as having an unpopular opinion. I completely reject that characterization of me. While I do believe in voicing my opinion, most of the time, people have used this description of me to deflect from the truth because it made them uncomfortable or forced them to look at the flaws in their own beliefs or actions. When that happens, I think it's important for us truth-tellers to embrace what I see as another facet of integrity—the ability to refrain from saying, "I told you so". If you genuinely desire to see people become better and embrace the truth over lies, there is no need to bask in a sense of self-righteousness when people finally see the truth you were telling. You don't have to rub anything in anybody's face because what will start happening over time, if you consistently tell the truth, is that people will start to believe and trust you as a source of truth, even if they don't like you and what you're saying. Dissenters won't respond as violently as they once did. They'll look at you and go on about their day, but you'll know that what you said landed because there's a history of you telling the truth.

That's one of the most satisfying rewards of telling the truth, not having to argue or get stressed out about what you're saying. I learned that in seventh grade, and ever since then, the truth has been my north star for life. People who know me have come to accept that if they ask me what happened, I'm going to give them the facts as I see them. That is not to say that the way I see things is always correct, but at least I can guarantee that what I say is what I saw. I saw my crush with a bag full of marijuana. I didn't want to tell on him. I knew what would come with that. I didn't want to be labeled a snitch, but I would not have been able to live with myself had I not said something. He was wrong, and thankfully, I had a set of personal boundaries that would not let me stay silent knowing that someone could be harmed as a result of my silence. More importantly, I realized that the only person I owed any accountability to was myself. I wanted to be able to look at myself in the mirror and confidently like who I see. I had already made a contract of integrity with myself, at the tender age of thirteen, that I wasn't willing to break, even at the risk of the negative social consequences I would face. That contract continues to guide me to this day. If I see someone being mistreated, I'm going to speak up. Is it hard sometimes? Yes. Does integrity and truth-telling sometimes cause discomfort and tension? Yes, but that's a risk I'm willing to take. The truth is worth it.

The final lesson I took from this memory, ironically, comes from The Mystery of Al Capone's Vault. Everyone was so invested in what might be hidden behind the walls of the Lexington Hotel. Thirty million people, who had never interacted with Al Capone and who would not benefit from anything being in that vault, took at least two hours of their time to watch the excavation, only to find absolutely nothing. My family was among that thirty million. I was literally at the brink of crisis, to the point that I tried to end my life, and my family was more interested in watching Geraldo Rivera go on a treasure hunt. That showed me that sometimes people are so invested in others' "vaults" to be opened that they miss what's being opened or revealed in their own lives. We seem to be hard-wired to expose secrets or dig up dirt on people, when most of us are living through messy situations and complications every day. That's a risky way to live because just as you are waiting on someone else's vault to be opened, there is sure to be someone waiting on yours to be opened as well. I hope my experience can be a reminder to you not to ignore the secrets, hidden struggles, or cries for help from those in your immediate circle because you're chasing the exposure of someone else. We all have issues that we're dealing with, enough to keep us busy until the end of time, so there is no need to go digging through someone else's vault, even if it is Al Capone. That's the lesson.

Open

How often do we hide deep inside our shells?
Cracked open enough to invite in tendrils of light
Closed enough to barricade ourselves within

Few open and close effortlessly enough with the current
The motion like a deep breath and slow exhalation
Most flutter without rhythm in random maddening
  intervals

Some lay closed and quiet for a lifetime

March 8, 2022

6

....

THE DEATH OF ANDY

Navigating adolescence is a tricky undertaking. Many of the memories and experiences I've shared with you happened around the same time, those tricky middle school years, between the ages of eleven and thirteen. The combination of hormones, the forming of social hierarchies among my peers, and the sheer uniqueness of the things I went through and survived had a significant impact on my rapidly developing personality and worldview. Additionally, the memories tied to my middle school years are important because they were the basis for some of my foundational beliefs and principles. Sharing these stories is cathartic as well as affirming, but reliving some of these events has also been painful. This next memory still evokes feelings of sadness and grief, but it's important and necessary to understanding who I am today. I mentioned all of this to warn you. This memory centers around death, the death of Andy.

My friend groups in middle school were interesting. Though I suffered from a little social awkwardness because of my propensity to be slightly overzealous about the things I knew, I did manage to have a close group of friends. I was still constantly struggling to find my own identity and accepting my indigo child tendencies, which left me in this weird kind of social no man's land. I didn't naturally fit into a clique because I didn't know who I was, so how could I know to which clique I belonged? As a result, I fell into a clique by default. We weren't a large group, five or six boys and girls.

The common trait among us was simply that we had known each other since kindergarten. That was it. Andy was in our little group. Andy was a skinny, towheaded boy with a great big smile. I don't know how everybody else felt about him, but to be quite honest, he irritated the hell out of me. That was normal, though. He just loved to annoy me. It was nothing big, just the normal, coming-of-age kind of annoyance where he would do and say some of the silly things adolescent boys were known for doing and saying, like taunting me with "I'm not touching you" while his hand is two inches away from my face. He would swear that he was never messing with me, but every time we crossed paths, he just couldn't resist hitting me. It's a common belief to think that when a boy acts like that, it's because he has a crush, but I don't think that was the case with Andy. He simply got pleasure out of seeing my frustration. That was our dynamic.

One day, we were on some sort of school field trip. We hadn't gone far, and I don't quite remember what we were doing. We could've been searching for arrowheads or fishing. Who knows? Whatever the occasion, Andy decided that this field trip would be yet another opportunity to work his magic on my nerves. He was especially worrisome that day. In addition to his usual taunts and quips, he kept stomping on the water next to my feet, splashing my feet. Well, after a while, I had had enough of his shenanigans. Completely out of character for my goodie-two-shoes persona, I got so upset with Andy that I cursed at him. I can't remember exactly what choice of explicative I flung out of my mouth, but I do remember the rest of my rant, declaring how annoying he was and how much I hated him. My tongue-lashing must have been pretty bad because I was punished and gladly suffered the consequences. I felt justified in my anger.

I went on about life as usual after that fight, not thinking much more about it, when just a few days later, one of my other friends from the kindergarten clique came up to me and flatly said, "Andy's dead." Though the messenger of this dark piece of news was also one of my close friends, it didn't immediately dawn on me which Andy he was talking about. There were a lot of Andys in our school, so I just replied how sad and unfortunate it was that Andy had passed. Just to be sure, I asked, "Which Andy?" My friend replied, "Our Andy!" Then it slowly started to set in that he was referring to *our* Andy, the same Andy that I'd known since kindergarten, that used to aggravate me to no end, to whom the last words I said were those of hate and disgust. *That* Andy was dead. I asked what happened to him, and our friend replied, "Nobody's really sure, but people are saying he put a shotgun in his mouth and pulled the trigger."

What?! I thought. This just seemed so strange, not the gun part. This was rural Florida. Every household had a shotgun. We all knew what to do with them, kids included. We knew how to shoot and hunt safely, and we had a healthy respect for guns. People just didn't kill themselves around here, especially not children, and especially not in this way.

It was right before the school day when I found out. By the time the actual school day started, the news had spread like wildfire. Though everyone was talking about it, there seemed to be a silence over the school, like a cloud of disbelief and sadness. There would be a small buzz of conversation and then just a lot of empty looks. We were all trying to process this at the same time, teachers, students, and faculty alike. Since these were the days before cell phones, the news seemed to hit pockets of the school and community in waves. Kids were excused to call home and alert their parents, and as the parents found out, they spread the news among the rest of the community. Soon, everyone knew, and every class was coping in their own way. Andy happened to be in my homeroom, along with a few more of the kids from our little clique. We were spread across two homerooms, so the ones who weren't in the homeroom with us and Andy were still processing the news. We were all in a state of shock and numbness at the same time. There we were in our homeroom, knowing Andy should be there too, but he wasn't.

The school day dragged on in what felt like a blurred state. We were going through the motions, but no one expected any learning or instruction to occur. After lunch, I remember sitting in another class that I shared with Andy, when our teacher began to check attendance. He started as usual, calling each child's name listed in his grade book as the students faintly repled, "Here." The room was eerily quiet, other than the teacher's voice and the kids' responses to their names, as those of us who were close to him tried to grapple with the fact that his chair was there, but he was not in it and never would sit in it again. Our instructor was robotically going through the names, and as he got to Andy's name, his mouth instinctively formed to say his name. He seemed to catch himself. His voice cracked as he said, "I'm sorry," and quickly exited the classroom. I know he didn't want us to see him break, but it was too late. We knew he was crying, at which time it felt like some invisible dam of sadness broke, and soon, every child in the room was engulfed in tears.

We carried on like that for several minutes, holding each other as we cried and released what felt like years of pain and grief. When our teacher rejoined the class, he gave us a few comforting words and opened the floor for anyone to ask questions or talk about what they were feeling. One by one, each student recalled what their last interactions and words with Andy were. I dared not share mine. It was enough for me to deal with the fact that I had been so unkind to him on my own. I couldn't possibly tell the whole class what I said to him. There were many silent moments and many spurts of conversation in which we all speculated what could have happened. Some kids thought he must have gotten into trouble with his parents or his grandfather. Nobody knew, and it seemed that the consensus was that, though we were curious as to his motivation for taking his life, we all had a larger concern. One of our friends, someone that many of us had known pretty much our whole lives, found himself so boxed in a corner, so stuck, so filled with desperation that he couldn't tell any of us or anyone that he needed help. Our Andy, who was so young and had so much of his life ahead of him, faced a darkness so thick that he felt his only way out was to put a shotgun in his mouth. How did that happen? How did none of us know he was going through anything?

The school offered counseling services to any kids who needed them. I didn't take advantage of that, though I probably should have. Instead, I went home and talked to my parents about it. I was met with very little comfort or condolences. Because my parents were never really present in anything that was happening to me, they didn't pay attention to anyone I knew. In response to me telling them what happened to Andy, they said, "Well, we don't really know the family, and you didn't really know him. What a shame, though." My dad then took the opportunity to stress to us how guns were not a toy, and he told us what he'd do to us if he ever caught us playing with his guns.

Andy's family had a closed-casket wake, and the school provided a bus for any children who wanted to attend the funeral. My parents forbade me from getting on that bus. They said that I was strong, and because I didn't really know him, I didn't need to go. It would be inappropriate for me to attend. Of all the students who knew him and of our little kindergarten clique, I was the only one who didn't attend his service. I'm sure everyone probably thought I was crazy, or mean, or cruel, or whatever, but my parents said I couldn't go. Though I was likely one of the children who needed to go to the service the most because of the haunting memory of our last interaction, I stayed behind at school, while the rest of my friends went to say goodbye. I had no closure. I never felt that I could apologize, and I couldn't work through my grief properly. Later on, I found a copy of his obituary in our town newspaper. I cut it out, put it in my little, middle school wallet, and carried it around with me for fifteen years or so. After transplanting that obituary from one wallet to another, it finally got so tattered and close to disintegration that I decided to burn it. As it burned, I held space for Andy's memory and for the grief that I still had for him. I hoped that he had forgiven me, hoped that he knew I didn't hate him, and neither did anybody else in his life.

On the surface, it probably seemed like my grief for Andy was similar to most of his friends. We were grieving the loss of his life and the fact that we didn't know he was hurting. It was more than that for me, though. Had I known what he was going through, I would have told him, "I'm so sorry that you never got to walk away from your pain and take a breath. I'm sorry that there wasn't anywhere you could go, be it outside, be it somewhere. I'm sorry you couldn't see just how much you mattered to all of us and how much it would hurt us to be without you."

I didn't know it then, but Andy's death would have an even greater impact on me later in life because I, too, would struggle with suicidal ideations. Andy's death gave me a firsthand glimpse of the wide-reaching effects of suicide. The whole aftermath, the unanswered questions, the pain, and the regret that other people feel never leave. I'm proof of that. I carried Andy's obituary around for years, and here I am writing about it now, decades later. It may seem like a quick fix, but the ripple effects on everyone around you last forever.

Years later, I was back in town for a short visit. I was in the local supermarket shopping, and I turned the corner and came in contact with what looked like the ghost of Andy. Luckily, I had been warned that this might happen. Otherwise, I would have seriously freaked out. It wasn't a ghost. It was Andy's little brother. He was a baby when Andy left us, and he grew up to be the spitting image of Andy. He had that same light blonde hair and big smile. I stopped in my tracks when I saw him. He didn't know who I was, but I knew exactly who he was as soon as I saw him. He said a cordial hello and walked on by. All I could do was hope he was getting the chance to live the life his brother didn't. I hoped he had joy, and if he ever found himself experiencing darkness, I hoped he had people to talk to and help pull him out of it. Then I thought about second chances, not necessarily for Andy, but for us. Whenever you get the chance to say something to someone, whether it's a compliment, an apology, or just a random nicety, say it. Now. Don't wait, and if you accidentally tell someone something you don't mean, go back and fix it right away. You never know. One unkind thing that you say to someone might seem insignificant, but if everyone in their life is saying something negative, you're adding to the weight that they already carry. Your one comment can be the one that breaks them.

There's one main lesson I took away from the death of Andy. I'm not perfect, and sometimes I do lash out as a result of a bad day or moment, but I never miss a chance to apologize. I liken this to my "breaking a lamp analogy." If you break a lamp, the minute you speak to the lamp's owner, you should confess. "I broke your lamp. I am so sorry I broke it. What can I do to make up for it? How can I fix it? How can I repay you for it? How can I get you a new lamp?" Don't hide that you broke it. Don't try to replace the lamp without telling them. Don't say, "I don't know who did it." Just admit that you broke the lamp. The truth and an apology are the best thing to do one hundred percent of the time. If I talk to someone and later realize that I said something, whether intentionally or unintentionally, that was hurtful, I'll call them up and say, "Hey, I just thought about an exchange we had where I think I said something that may have come off in a hurtful way. If so, I'm sorry because I didn't mean that." Sometimes the person says, "Yeah, it was weird. Thank you for apologizing," and sometimes they say, "No, I didn't think about that at all, but thanks for apologizing anyway." That's all because of Andy. Maybe, in the grand scheme of things, what I said to him wasn't important at all, but that was the lesson I learned. Words matter, and the same way kindness can change someone's day, so can negativity. I won't let negative words be the last thing I say to anyone. That's a vow I made to Andy. That's how I honor his memory. That's the lesson.

Puzzle

Born unplanned—this indigo child
A puzzle piece not matching any open spots

Curiosity from day one—why? But why?
Creativity its equal partner in mischievousness

Green eyes whose shade shifts with emotions
Radiant smile shared with anyone watching

A child most comfortable in the bosom of nature
Meandering blissfully through her world

Avid mind most like a sponge with endless thirst
Reading, asking, questioning, learning, probing

A lover of the truth, of kindness, of love
Music, animals, trees, colors, water, people

Yet a puzzle piece placed in the wrong box
Constantly set aside on the edges of the table

Watching from the perimeter—trying to matter
Holding everyone accountable for their truths

This indigo child spoke to the moon, the stars
Reaching out to the universe for guidance

Several times life was almost cut short
By choice, by malfeasance, by accident

Abandoned more than once, this puzzle piece
As a child, as an adolescent, as an adult

Yet the light never truly went out behind that smile
Those eyes still shifted with the light

Reinventing, rediscovering, learning, moving, building
Loving, birthing, raising, forgiving, persevering

The larger puzzle perhaps isn't meant to be solved
Perhaps it's meant to be admired for the individual
  pieces

This unique puzzle piece, this indigo child
This light, these eyes, this smile—this me.

April 5, 2022

7

....

INDIGO LATCH KEY KIDS

During World War II, a new social phenomenon began to appear across households in America. More and more children were being left at home alone while their parents worked. This phenomenon gave birth to the term "latchkey kids," and the generation that is most often referred to as the first generation of latchkey kids is Generation X. The rise in latchkey kids can be directly attributed to the increase in divorce and the societal acceptance of the notion as well as the number of working mothers increasing. Whatever the case, Gen-Xers are often thought of as the least parented generation. Many studies have been conducted on the positive and negative effects of growing up as a latchkey kid. Possible positive consequences are learning independence and responsibility. Some of the potential negative consequences are loneliness, boredom, fear, academic underachievement, drug and alcohol abuse, accidental injuries, and strained parent-child relationships.

Another social concept that became popular as Generation X was growing up was that of the indigo child. The term indigo child describes a child with special abilities that are believed to be supernatural. The New Age beliefs of the 1970s helped to formulate this ideology. Characteristics of such children are that they are intuitive, sensitive, strong-willed, creative, and empathetic. These children were believed to have a proclivity for learning, positivity, the advancement of society, and just innate curiosity.

They were supposed to learn differently and behave differently. They were called indigo because their auras were supposedly indigo, which was a different color than most people. The theory was that these children would inevitably, collectively or individually, move society to be better, live better, and break through some of the negative social norms. That was the positive description of the indigo child. There was a negative side to these children as well. A child who is too curious, hyperactive, uncontrollable, and has problems with authority is the negative description of an indigo child. Some say the concept of indigo children is pseudoscientific and was just a way to label neurodivergent children or any child who didn't fit the most common diagnostic criteria at a time when we weren't as knowledgeable about differing levels of cognitive capabilities. Either way, I fit the bill.

I don't ever remember being formally diagnosed as such, but I had all of the common traits of an indigo child. I was tested for the gifted program very early in my life and was told that I didn't quite make it, only to later on, be retested and found to be so. I could read and speak two languages by the time I entered Kindergarten. I learned subjects and concepts very quickly and tested very well. I also learned to speed read at a very young age, and my favorite word was "why". I had several different characteristics that were unique and showed signs of above-average intelligence. For example, I had an innate ability to recognize patterns and see abnormalities quickly. I did very well on those pattern recognition tests they used to give kids, or those little exercises where the viewer would be asked to look at two pictures and find the differences. I could do those at lightning speed very early in my life. I was also observant. I could take a walk in the woods and see movement where no one else would see it. I was extremely hypersensitive to change or disruption. Those traits, if nurtured, can be beneficial to a child in promoting curiosity and ingenuity. These traits, if not nurtured, could be seen as annoying or mischievous. Children who ask many questions can sometimes be seen as challenging authority, which is not always the case. They just have a desire to know things.

Whereas there was no formal way to label me as an indigo child, there is no question of whether I fit the characteristics of a latchkey kid. I am the epitome of the latchkey kid phenomenon. A couple of times throughout my life, in all grades at all points in time, my family has forgotten to pick me up. It started when I was really little, and it did not end in high school. They would just forget, and when they remembered, I would have been sitting somewhere for hours. When I was really little, in elementary school, they would pick me up from school, take me to the office, and let me play in the back. They'd tell me to be quiet and not to get in the way. As I got a little older and they forgot me a couple of times, they pivoted away from bringing me to the office. I think they realized that since the school wasn't too far from home, they could just give me a key, and I could go home. My parents did try a couple of times to have someone there to watch us, but it usually ended up just being me and my brother, when he remembered to come home. My brother was a player. He was out in the streets, being with the ladies, doing who knows what, so I was just home alone.

Every day after school, I walked home, which was right across the street, so it wouldn't take me a long time. We had one of those business phones, the ones that had the phone line at the office that also rang at home. Once I got home, I would punch the one line, call the office, say, "I'm home," and hang up. Then, I'd do my homework, eat a snack, and entertain myself. It was a very lonely existence. If you add on the fact that I had all these questions, curiosity, and information I wanted to explore, being an indigo latchkey kid could seem like torture. There was nothing to do, no one to ask questions, no one guiding the stimulation that I needed. I had this desperation for learning and experimentation that was festering, lying dormant every time I came home to an empty house. I won't trivialize the danger of children being home alone at any point in history, but just to put some context to the times in which I was coming home alone, it was the late seventies and early eighties in Northern Florida. Do you know what else was happening in the late seventies and early eighties in Northern Florida? Does the name Ted Bundy mean anything to you? I'm not saying that I was in any danger of being abducted by Ted

Bundy, one of the United States' most infamous serial killers, but think of what the social climate must have been like at the time. Imagine what the news was reporting around that time and the palpable fear and paranoia that must have been on the minds of young women, and there I was, a lanky pre-teen who looked older than she was, meandering alone through the woods on any given afternoon. Anything or anyone could have done me harm, but I'd rather risk the possibility of danger in the surrounding woods than the chaos that existed at my house.

There is no question that the woods surrounding my house and school were not the safest location for me. However, being at home didn't feel safe for me at the time, either. By this time in my life, I fully realized I was the odd man out at home. My brother, my sister, and I were butting heads more often. My father was completely broken at this point, so he and my mother were constantly at odds. There was also more drinking at home at this time, so it just didn't feel safe. There was more belonging and more safety outside of the home than inside. On top of that, incessant thoughts of being unwanted filled my mind. *No one has time for you. No one wants to interact with you. No one cares about you.* I know there are and were so many children who had to suffer much worse, not having food, adequate shelter, facing physical abuse, etc., but being left to my own devices so often felt like neglect to me. It was. It was psychological and emotional neglect. It wasn't about not having food. I would get home, cook, and eat. It's not about having a place to sleep or a way to wash myself or dress myself. I had all of those things, but there was no psychological or emotional connection. No one asked me about my schoolwork. No one could help me with my schoolwork. There wasn't any concern about whether I got an "A" or not. The only thing that seemed to matter was whether I was the best in my class. If I were the best, great. That's all they cared about. They didn't care about the context. They didn't care about what I was learning. They didn't care about what I was doing. In my frustrated attempt to secure the much-needed attention from my parents, I overperformed at school. I was the standard overachiever. I'd get the highest grades possible, just so I could come home and say, "Look!" hoping for some form of validation and praise, to get an unenthusiastic, "Ok". Luckily, academic excellence was my outlet. Can you imagine if I decided to misbehave and get into trouble as a way to gain their attention? Regardless of what I did or didn't do, there was still this lack of connection with my parents that created an extreme chasm of loneliness and isolation that I struggled throughout my childhood to fill.

One thing that my mother did that ended up being a lifeline for me during this time was signing me up for the *Weekly Reader* Book Club. If you're not familiar with *Weekly Reader*, it was a weekly newspaper, started in 1928, and distributed in classrooms that encouraged children to read newspapers. By the time I was in elementary school, *Weekly Reader* had added another aspect to its circulation–*Weekly Reader* Book Club. My mom signed me up for it, so I began receiving two books every two weeks. I would devour those books. I read every single one of them. The books became my escape. I don't quite remember how long I was in the club, but I have 136 books. I still have every single book to this day.

Once I read all of the *Weekly Reader* books, I started reading any and every book that was around the house. Then I started reading my father's medical books. Nobody said anything, so I just kept reading. We didn't have the internet then, so books were the most accessible way for me to get exposure to information, which is something I desperately craved. You would think I would be a parent's dream – a kid who loved to read? The truth is, though, my incessant reading was just a coping mechanism for my extreme loneliness. My life was an unremarkable exercise in rep-etition. Every day was the same. Wake up. Eat breakfast. Walk to school. Finish the school day. Walk home. Do homework. Find something to read. Go outside. Read in the woods. Come back. Eat dinner. Go to bed. Repeat the next day. It was this quiet, mundane, lonely experience.

Because of this isolated routine, anytime I was around people or any-one remotely close to my age, I would bombard them with questions and conversation. People were annoyed with me, I'm sure. They started call-ing me Smart Alec and a know-it-all, which wasn't exactly great for social currency. I couldn't figure out why they were annoyed. I would constantly ask, "Did you know this?" and "Don't you want to know about that?" Their answer was always, "No, we don't want to know." That's when I started my tradition of telling fun facts. I would randomly tell people, "Fun fact..." and then give some obscure piece of information. I'm almost fifty-three now, and I still do that. I loved learning and sharing new information. I've learned how to temper it over the years, so as not to come off pretentious, but I still do it because I still love learning and sharing knowledge. I believe that when we have a love of learning, we can either turn it off and try to be cool, or we can embrace it and be joyful about learning. I don't know when gaining knowledge became bad, but I'd like to make it good again. After all, knowledge is still power.

I can't speak for all latchkey kids, but many of us suffered a quiet sadness of learning new information at school and being desperate to tell someone, or having something really exciting or really bad happen at school and needing to vent at home, only to find that no one is there to listen. I've found, through my own experience as a latchkey kid and also being a parent myself, that one of the most important connection points for any child is the moment they get home or the moment they get in the car from pickup. In those first fifteen or twenty minutes, they need someone to talk to and unload the baggage from the day, whether good or bad. That need starts as we're children, even babies. Think about it. A baby is crawling around on the floor. They find something new, and they do one of three things, probably all three: He or she picks it up, puts it in his or her mouth, and then shows it to you. They don't even have words yet, but they want to share what they've discovered and found. We seem to be hard-wired to do that. We want to feel, taste, observe, and immediately go, "Look what I found!"

There are several impactful experiences that I wanted to share with my family, only to find that they were not available to listen to me. In eighth grade, for example, we had this program called Kid City. It was a community of eighth graders. It was a privilege to be chosen for this program. If you were really lucky, and you excelled academically and in leadership, you could be elected as a leader in Kid City. To add to that, if you ranked in the top twenty academic achievers of one of the subjects, you would also be selected to sit in a very special row right in front of the teacher. Everybody wanted to be in that row, and I was no exception. As I mentioned before, I tried hard to perform well academically, so not only was I in the top twenty, but I was also in the top ten of academic achievers in my class. Consequently, I was elected to be a Kid City monitor, and I got to sit in that coveted front row. I was proud of that, but sadly, there was no one to share it with when I got home.

Most of middle school followed that same trend. Impactful moments were happening all the time, and I longed to share the details with my folks, but they just couldn't be bothered. In fact, my home life was getting more chaotic and fractured by the day. That special bond I had with my dad was almost non-existent by this point. I think one of the biggest issues was the fact that we stayed in this small town after his medical license was revoked, as opposed to moving away. As a result, he found himself sort of lost, broken, and trapped in this town. He also found himself at complete odds with my mom, and I could feel them breaking apart. All of this was going on during the school year, and then the summer came. A time that would usually be filled with excitement and adventure was a nightmare for me that year because I got my period. This wasn't the typical first-period experience, either. This thing wreaked havoc on me. I was hemorrhaging blood like a fountain. My dad, still clinging to his shattered medical career, listened to my mother's fear of transfusions and chose to treat me at home, though I needed to be hospitalized. I spent the entire summer in bed, and I'm honestly surprised I didn't die from the blood loss. That seemed to be the final nail in the coffin for my dad's relationship with me and my family. The fact that he couldn't nurse me back to health must have been a final blow to his self-esteem. After that, he started having more affairs and looking for work outside of our town, and his and my mom's relationship completely fell apart. At the same time, Mom and I were also at each other's throats every day. We just couldn't see eye to eye about anything. The next thing I knew, my dad moved to South Florida, supposedly for the betterment of the family, and everybody else just seemed to be in survival mode.

Since everybody in my family was doing their own thing at this time, my needs went from mildly neglected to grossly neglected. I felt like I was flailing. No support. No one talked to me. My dad was gone, and in my eyes, he was the only one who really cared about me. Now I had no one. It was an awful time. My brother finished high school and went to live with my dad. I'm not sure how to describe my parents' marriage at that point. They weren't divorced, but they weren't calling themselves separated either. They claimed to be trying to make it work, just with my dad at one end of the state and my mom on the other. We were all just pretending to be a family. We were far from it. Somehow, I managed to get through ninth grade in the International Baccalaureate program at my school in North Florida, when all of a sudden, my parents made the decision that we would reunite by all moving to South Florida. This move was a huge disruption in my life, which no one seemed to take into consideration, and that began the complete and total end to anyone remembering that I existed, let alone that I had an education to complete. It seemed like they never missed an opportunity to show me that I wasn't important enough to be given a nurturing environment in which to grow and develop.

Though we moved hours away from the first house where I became intimately acquainted with the loneliness and neglect that accompany a latchkey childhood, my parents brought that same neglect to our new home in South Florida. They were still forgetting about me, and this time I couldn't just walk home. One particular incident sticks out in my memory as an especially dangerous instance of them leaving me with no way to get home. I was only fifteen when I enrolled in my first new school. Not only did I not know anybody at school, but I also did not know anything about the community around it, especially not how to get back to my house. One day, I somehow got stuck at school after dismissal. I found a nearby payphone, called my house, and let my mom know that I needed a ride home, emphasizing that I don't know my way around town, so this was slightly urgent. My mom then told me that she was sending one of her friends' sons to come pick me up because no one else was available. Yes, you read that right—my mom's friend's son. His name was Armando, which, I guess, was helpful to know, but he was a complete stranger to me. An hour after that phone call, and three hours after school was dismissed, a young man pulled up to the school. He rolled down his window and yelled, "Hey, I'm Armando, Armandito's son, and I'm here to pick you up." All I could think was, *This guy is going to kill me.* Sheepishly, I replied, "Ok" and got into the car. Armando then looked at me and commented on how frightened I looked. I respectfully explained to him that I was only nervous because I didn't know him. Thankfully, he understood and explained that his aunt was my mom's friend, and she asked him to pick me up as a favor to my mom. He asked if I knew how to get to my house, and of course, I didn't. I did have the address, though, and fortunately, Armando knew the city well enough to get me back home. Remember, this was before the days of GPS or Google Maps on your phone. Luckily, Armando was nice and got me home safely, but that wasn't the last time I had to get a ride from other people because no one at my house realized or remembered that I needed transportation home. Sometimes, I rode the bus. Other times, I would just beg someone else to hitch a ride. Either way, these experiences were constant reminders that nothing had changed for me with this move. In North Florida, I was completely on my own in middle school, and after the move, I soon realized I was completely on my own as a high school student as well.

In addition to reminding me that I was still very much alone, the move to South Florida also almost ruined my chances at academic success. At my old school, I was in the International Baccalaureate program, and had I been blessed with parents who were invested in my academic progress, I would have been transferred to a school with a comparable IB program. Unfortunately, my reality was far from that. The first new school I entered had no IB program, no magnet program, no semblance of any accelerated track that could challenge a student like me. There was nothing particularly special about the school, and even if there was, I was enrolled too late to participate. That didn't matter, though, because midway through my year at this new school, my family moved again, and I started at yet another new school, again, too late to be placed into any academically rigorous courses. My folks were too busy with the chaos of their own lives to take any interest in my progress, and they were not about to take time to go to the school and fix it. That's when that voice that reminded me that no one was coming to save me in middle school after the drug scandal, once again reminded me that I was going to have to be my own advocate and take control of my educational journey. I rolled up my sleeves and got myself enrolled in Advanced Placement courses. I worked diligently for the next two years and managed to earn about twenty-seven college credits before graduating from high school, all on my own. I also went through the entire college application process on my own, securing several different acceptances and even a few scholarship offers from some competitive schools with good reputations.

Though my parents took no interest in my education before I was faced with the decision of which college I would attend, they made a point to insert themselves in my life and insist that I enroll at the University of Miami, even though some of my other options were less expensive and were accompanied by scholarships. They made a case for me going to this particular school because my brother was there and because I could live at home. I'm not sure why my educational pursuits suddenly became a matter of importance, but I eventually capitulated and enrolled at The U. That interest didn't last long, though. Soon, the same lack of support I experienced throughout my middle school and high school years followed me well into college. During my second year at the University of Miami, I wrote a poem to celebrate women and the diversity of women of every color as an entry to a poetry contest the school was hosting. I submitted it in collaboration with another student. He entered the photography portion, and I, the poetry. We made a calendar for which my partner took the pictures, and I wrote a stanza for every month of the calendar. Each stanza represented women and the diversity of women in every color, shape, size, etc. This project meant a lot to me, and the time taken to complete it was a major sacrifice. As a former latch-key kid, I was now navigating college on my own. My parents had now basically left me to fend for myself after their divorce, which meant I had no way to pay for school. After freshman year, I took a sabbatical from my studies, got a job, and re-entered college while working nights and weekends to pay for my degree. I had a lot going on, so finding out that we had won this calendar photo/poetry contest was a highlight of my matriculation. I was proud of that, as I should have been, but like my eighth-grade experience with Kid City, my family was nowhere to be found when I wanted to share this accomplishment. Though I was years past that eighth-grade memory, the pain of that moment came rushing back at the realization that I was still battling the neglect of an unsupportive family. Same problem, different location.

I have learned several things as a result of being a latchkey kid. The curiosity and need to share that we develop as children doesn't disappear as we grow older. If anything, that need gets stronger. We also don't forget how it feels if we're not fortunate enough to have someone with whom to share our findings. I never forgot how it felt to come home alone with no one to talk to or share my day, so I made it a point, when I became a parent, to try as hard as possible to make sure my children never felt that same isolation. Whenever I picked my kids up from school, extracurricular activities, or any time I hadn't seen them in a while, I always asked, "What's new?". I still ask them that now, even though they're adults. My daughter is engaged and planning a wedding. Because I know wedding plans have the potential to get extremely stressful, I am even more intentional about asking her about the new things she's experiencing. Just recently, I called her and my future son-in-law and asked, "What new and exciting thing happened today?" Like clockwork, they began to gush about visiting a wedding venue and enjoying a great meal that day. The conversation was a mix of special and mundane, but I value these moments and am very intentional about creating space for them to share. I always want to make sure that the people I care about know that I care about their lives and everything they're experiencing. It's a small gesture, but it makes a huge impact.

The act of feeling heard and having a safe person just to release the baggage of your day is important to children and adults alike. Many people want to feel like their life and the things they are experiencing and learning are important. How do we do that in our daily lives? How do we create that space for someone else to release their day? How do we reject our natural inclination to complain or bemoan the unpleasant things that happen to us and consider that those we love or care about might also want to unburden their thoughts and feelings? I think it starts with realizing that other people want to share their stories the same way we want to share ours. While it is important to make sure you have someone to share your day's occurrences and resulting feelings, it's equally important to create that same space for someone else. When catching up with someone after a while, try saying, "I'm so excited to see you. Tell me something that happened to you today." If they respond that nothing good or exciting happened today, but something bad happened, be able to say, "Okay, share that, then." Be clear. I'm not advising you to give advice, counsel, or become anybody's therapist. Just lend a listening ear. So many people need that these days, but they don't know how to articulate that they just need to unload. Hopefully, after reading this, you will be more intentional about asking people to share their day and mean it. I'll always be a proponent of this practice because I spent a lifetime growing up with no one willing to hear all of my new and exciting things. We've got to do better for our children and our loved ones. Be the recipient of someone else's new and exciting news. It doesn't take money, and it doesn't take effort. It just takes time. You'd be surprised how much of a difference it can make in your loved ones' lives, especially the children. That's the lesson.

Together

I hear from within, a distant rumble
It echoes through the valleys in my mind
Something has stirred the woman awake
On the outside—size and shape and looks mature
On the inside—soft and supple and green

At night I wrestle with her presence
Can the child and the woman cohabitate?
She promises to keep me and protect me
In return, she must show through and express herself

I slowly let go of my childish antics
I feel the woman in me now—her fears, needs and
*   desires*
How strange she feels—yet so much still like the child
She has kept her promise

January 1991

8

....

LOSING MY MAIDENHEAD

I lost my maidenhead in the most unusual, ridiculous, non-sexual way possible. If you think that was a jarring way to start a chapter, just know it was purposeful. Conversations about sex can get uncomfortable sometimes, so what better way to start this memory than just jumping right in? If you're not familiar with the term, maidenhead, it's an archaic English word that refers to a woman's virginity. It's the non-medical term for the hymen, the thin piece of tissue that surrounds the vaginal opening. It is a common-held belief that an unbroken hymen is an indicator of virginity in women because many women experience bleeding during their first experience of vaginal intercourse after the hymen is broken, resulting in the loss of their maidenhead. It doesn't always happen like this, though. I lost my maidenhead at nine and didn't even know it.

Part of the uniqueness of my childhood is that, though I had an older sister, all of my hand-me-downs came from my older brother. I outgrew my sister at an alarming rate. She's barely five-three as an adult, so you can imagine how tall she was during adolescence. I'm five-nine now, but at age nine, I was already taller than five-three. Being that puberty hadn't quite kicked in around this age, my physical makeup was more akin to my brother's physical structure than my sister's, so when he outgrew something, it was handed down to me. Clothes, toys, bikes, it didn't matter. If my brother outgrew it, I got it. Our physical makeup wasn't the only thing we had in common, either. I was the poster child for tomboys back then. I rode bikes, motorcycles, and horses. I hiked, dove into ponds, and explored the woods to my heart's content. By today's standards, I would just be seen as an active, outdoorsy girl, but in the late seventies and eighties, I was labeled a tomboy, basically because I didn't like to wear skirts and participated in what was then considered to be boy things. I'm so glad we've made a little bit of progress in that area and no longer categorize activities based on gender identity as much as we did back then. I was just a girl who liked to be in nature.

My bike was one of the many items passed down to me from my brother once he got too big for it. One day, my brother and I were outside enjoying an afternoon of bike-riding. We normally weren't allowed to ride bikes away from home, and since our mom was home that day, we kept our bike-riding contained to the driveway. Had she not been home, we would have been wildly roaming the highways and byways of our neighborhood without a care in the world. However, that day, we followed the rules, and we were having an amazing time, even if we were confined to the driveway. Now, if you know anything about bikes, you know that the main difference between a girl's bike and a boy's bike is that pesky bar between the handlebars and the seat. Boys' bikes have the bar that extends straight across, while girls' bikes have the bar that slants or curves downwards. I never understood why that bar was there, and I would soon have a reason never to forget just how dangerous that bar could be.

Many factors created perfect conditions for an inevitably gruesome accident. First, our driveway was shaped like a semicircle and had a moderately steep incline to it. It was long and wide enough to do some decent riding, but it was not long and wide enough to do the death-defying tricks my brother and I were attempting that day. Next, though we lived on a rural road that was paved, it was still very busy. Cars were passing all the time, so we had to be extra careful. We also had to make sure that we attempted all of our tricks in the direction of the house. Doing tricks toward the road put us in danger of landing on the road and getting hit by one of the many cars, pickups, or semi-trucks that passed at any given moment. Despite all of the dangerous factors, we took the necessary precautions and proceeded to perform these elaborate tricks, when out of nowhere, BAM! My brother and I crashed right into each other. It was a massive collision. Bikes and appendages were flying and intertwining everywhere. We just ate it. My brother's bike was mangled, and we both had visible scrapes and bruises everywhere. It was so awful that passersby who witnessed the collision stopped to check if we were ok. I don't remember my brother's condition, but I was not ok. When we collided, I slid off the seat, landing with what felt like the force of ten men, directly onto that bar. This is why that bar doesn't make sense to me, because if I had been a boy, my testicles would have been damaged for life after that. Not being a boy didn't save me from being permanently affected, though, because I bruised everything around my vagina–inner labia, everything. I also lost my maidenhead.

We finally untangled the mess that was our bikes and limped slowly to the house to assess and tend to the wounds we had just amassed. My brother immediately retrieved the iodine from the medicine cabinet and began treating his wounds. I, however, was experiencing a different type of pain that I knew iodine wouldn't help. I went to the bathroom, found blood all over my panties, and thought, *Oh, I'm in trouble now.* Like any quick-thinking nine-year-old, I panicked and decided it would be best to hide the bloody panties, all the way down to the bottom of the laundry basket. No one would find them there. Of course, that very same weekend, my mother was busy pulling all the laundry out. Out of nowhere, she came running into my room in a panic, grabbed my arm, dragged me into her room, locked the door, and proceeded to scare me to death by frantically declaring, "I found this underwear. You need to tell me who has touched you! What has happened?" I responded, matching my mom's panic, "Touched me. What do you mean, 'touched me'? You've touched me, and my dad's touched me, and my sister touched me, and the dog has touched me." I went on and on listing people or things that touched me, until my mom stopped me and again said, "No. I mean, who has TOUCHED you?" She emphasized "touched" that time. Still clueless, I just stared at her blankly, and she exclaimed, "Down there!". I questioned, "Down where?" Mom finally pointed to the evidence in the laundry basket, and it clicked for me. I immediately tensed up and asked, "Am I in trouble?" She assured me that I wasn't in trouble, while still emphatically urging me to tell her what happened. "We had a bike accident, and the bikes are messed up because we hid the bikes. The bikes and, and then and you know, his bike is all messed up. My bike and." I rambled on incoherently for about thirty more seconds leaving my mom no more informed about what happened than when she first pulled me into the room. The whole encounter played out like an episode of one of the family sitcoms from the days of Thanks Goodness It's Friday or TGIF programming on ABC. We were both saying words, but nothing was making sense to either of us. Finally, after about twenty minutes of interrogating and putting pieces together, my mother went from fear and panic to laughter. I went from anxiety and fear of punishment to complete confusion because, though Mom seemed to understand me, I still didn't know what she was talking about. "So," she said, "You're telling me you crashed into your brother on the bike, hit the bar, and now it hurts down there?" The realization that I was not going to be punished for this started to settle in, so I relaxed a little. "Yeah, it hurts bad. I came down on it really hard, Mom, and then it bled. I thought I was going to get into trouble because the bikes are all ruined." I pulled up my jeans and showed her all the bruises and scratches on my legs. I did the same for my arms and elbows. She looked at all the scratches and gave no response. The interesting thing is that I don't know if she believed me or not, but she never said anything else about it. She didn't take me to my dad or any other doctor to get checked out. She just threw the underwear away and never brought it up again.

Fast forward about ten or eleven years, I was twenty or twenty-one and engaged to be married. Like a good Catholic girl, I was still a virgin. I had done things, fooled around, over-the-clothes activity, but I had not yet had vaginal intercourse. Believe it or not, even with a doctor for a dad, I knew little to nothing about sex. I learned about tampons from conversations with friends. That information was questionable, though, because I didn't even start using them until later in adult life. There was a common misconception among my peers that using tampons disqualified one from being a virgin. How ridiculous, right? The extent of my sex education was being told that nothing was to go into my vagina. It seemed to me that the most important aspect of sex was to know that virginity was sacred, and if you let it go before marriage, you couldn't wear white to your wedding. That's it.

By this time, my fiancé and I had been engaged for almost a year, and constant pressure seemed to exist to have sex. He complained incessantly about how ridiculous the concept of waiting was since we were already engaged. He would say things like, "If you loved me, this wouldn't be a problem. We're engaged. You bought your dress. Marriage is imminent, so what's the big deal?" According to him, the paperwork and the ceremony had very little to do with how we felt, so I should just go ahead and have sex with him. That logic or just his persistence wore me down because one day, I decided that since my fiancé and I were officially engaged and had begun planning for the wedding, it was time for me to take that step. I wanted to have sex. The night that I decided to go through with it, I was house-sitting for someone, and I invited my fiancé over. I don't know what made me decide on this night other than opportunity. We had this house to ourselves, and since I still lived at home with my parents, the possibility of us having a space to ourselves again was slim to none. I got busy setting the scene. I cooked dinner for him. Candles were lit, and the atmosphere was set for this romantic occasion. Although I had no idea what I was doing or what to expect, I was sure that this was about to be a special and romantic night. I felt very grown-up and sophisticated. I was sorely mistaken.

After dinner, things started to escalate physically. It was awkward. I was awkward. I clearly didn't know what I was doing, and looking back on it, I don't think he knew what he was doing either. He was just used to saying what he wanted and getting it. We got to a point in our makeout session where a decision had to be made. Will we, or won't we? I wasn't ready, and neither was my body. I quickly learned that when my body isn't ready, there is no lubrication, and when there is no lubrication, there is pain. For that reason, I backed out. I just didn't feel comfortable and decided that I didn't want to go through with it. Immediately, my fiancé went on this persuasive campaign to change my mind. "We're engaged. I came all the way out here. You're house-sitting, and we're all alone. No one's gonna bother us." He threw out every coercive technique he could think of to cajole me into giving him what he wanted. After several minutes of unsuccessful attempts at getting me to relent, he must have just decided he didn't need my permission. Though I was adamant that I didn't want to have sex after all, my fiancé forced himself on me. There wasn't a word for it back then, but it was the equivalent of date or spousal rape today. It was horrible and most certainly not the experience I wanted. I didn't give my virginity away. It was taken, and by someone who was supposed to love me, the man I was supposed to marry.

Given the loss of my maidenhead at nine years old, it should come as no surprise to you that unlike many women's first experience with vaginal intercourse, there was no blood. It surprised my fiancé, though. He then began to question the validity of virginity. This man had audacity. "You said you were a virgin," he barked. "I was," I replied, "until now." "Well, you're lying," he shot back, " because virgins bleed." The nerve of this man, to assault me and then feign indignation at the thought of me lying to him about being a virgin. After reiterating that he didn't believe me and accusing me of sleeping with someone else, he said that we would talk about it later and left in a fit of anger. There I sat, in this big house with two beautiful Siamese cats and my thoughts. The rest of the night was just such a weird, awful expanse of time. All I could do was think about the fact that I waited this long to give myself to someone I loved, only for him to accuse me of giving myself to someone else and hurl insults of impurity at me. The added violation and trauma of the assault increased the level of disappointment for the evening. I even thought about all the other times I had been in sexually tense situations, whether it was with my fiancé or the only other boyfriend I had, and how I had fought so hard to refrain from going all the way. I would think to myself during those times,

I can't possibly go any further because I need to be a good girl. I felt cheated, like I should have allowed myself to go there, then at least, maybe I would have enjoyed it. I questioned if my first time would have been different with somebody else. I began to doubt myself and wish that I had given in before, when I was in control, when I wanted it. What was the point in waiting if I was just going to end up being assaulted?

Needless to say, that relationship didn't make it. That experience, though traumatic, isn't the main focus of this memory. The focus of this memory is the idea of virginity and sexual autonomy. For my whole life, up until that night, I had been saving myself. I had listened to all the religious rhetoric and societal messages about virginity and sex, which made it seem like my virginity wasn't even mine. It was something that I was supposed to reserve for somebody else. In the moments after this assault, however, I realized I had been looking at my virginity through the eyes of others, the religion of my childhood, my family, my culture, and my future husband. It didn't belong to any of them, though. My virginity was mine, and I should have been empowered to do whatever I wanted with it. The same is true for you. Your virginity is yours. Don't make disclaimers about it. Don't make justifications about it. It should never belong to anyone else in terms of selling it, marrying it off, or assigning it value. All of the things that we do now and have done for centuries with women's virginity are just wrong. It's like we've allowed society to build this fragile little glasshouse of women's purity. We romanticize it and put it on this pedestal, but the house has a weak foundation or no foundation at all because we don't properly teach young people about their bodies or consent. We avoid conversations about foreplay. We don't tell them what happens with acceptance. We don't tell them what needs to happen to get their bodies ready. As a result, it becomes extremely difficult to create a truly, physically, emotionally accepting moment for sex to be pleasurable, for sex to be happy, for sex to truly live up to the expectations we have in our minds, because we don't know how to do it. Without proper education, sex will never result in that romanticized, Hollywood (fake) orgasm if people aren't taught what to do. Let's be honest. We're setting people up for disappointment at the least or putting them in harm's way at the most. We're preparing people, mainly women, for unpleasant experiences, after which they immediately form negative feelings toward sex. What does that do? It makes them not want to do it again because they aren't experiencing pleasure, and that creates the perfect environment for a violation like the one I experienced.

Look, if you're reading this, especially if you're a woman, and you haven't experienced sex, know this. If you want to save yourself until you get married, great, but do it because you want to, not because you're saving it for a future spouse. It's still your body, and your value as a woman, wife, or partner is not affected by the state of your hymen. While you wait, do yourself a favor and educate yourself as much as possible. Talk to some sex positive women, and get comfortable with your body. Most importantly, get comfortable with your perception and expectations surrounding sex and sexual autonomy. Though my body has been through some trauma surrounding the state of my maidenhead, there is a semi-sweet irony to all of this. The breaking of the hymen can happen in many different ways. It can be broken during exercise, accidents, gynecological exams, or even tampon use. Furthermore, the idea that an unbroken hymen is an indicator of virginity doesn't hold up. Mine broke because of a biking accident. Does that mean that I lost my virginity to a bicycle? If so, then no man took my virginity, and the man who thought he took my virginity didn't. I choose to see that as poetic irony, because he didn't deserve it. Regardless of the technicality of the whole situation, the memory of this just reminds me of the power in sexual autonomy and understanding one's self-worth outside of the value society has placed on sexual purity. No one's value lies in their sexual history. Anything to the contrary is absurd. That's the lesson.

Rescued

I stand on a narrow precipice called loneliness
I have only the comfort of the wind pressing me against
* the rock*
In the distance I hear the faint footsteps of a man
My mind stretches and strains to recognize the sound

Slowly, against the pressure, I lift my eyes to the edge
* above me*
He walks so close, yet I cannot touch him
My soul sits upon my breast anxiously
I realize it is the step of a friend

The wind fights me and tears my words from the air
My tears no sooner form, than they are dried to a salty
* grain*
He comes closer in my direction, in desperation I turn
* onto the stone*
My fingers claw at it, my mind and body unite in the
* struggle to climb*

His steps recede but a few paces
My heart stops, my entire being freezes in time and
* space*
He leaves me, he leaves me here to hang suspended
Not dead, but constantly dying

When all of a sudden I hear as he stretches onto the
   ground
He has not left me, he merely closes our distance as he
   leans over me
I see his soul reach for mine as our eyes meet
Warmly, I feel him caress my cheek with his hand

Inch by inch, he raises me and enfolds me in his
   tenderness
From shaky precipice, I find myself on soft downy
   ground
Security is wrapped around me as his arms envelop me
This man, this friend has saved me

Without the artifice of a rope, he secures me
As he revives my stone-cold features
Sense oozes into my limbs
I am alive, and warm and loved

January 20, 1994

9

....

GO JOHNNY, GO!

"Johnny B. Goode" by Chuck Berry—depending on the decade in which you experienced childhood or young adulthood, the lyrics to this song might evoke a sense of nostalgia for many reasons. If you're a child of the fifties, you might think of Chuck Berry, a pioneer in American music, known to most as the father of rock n roll. If you're a child of the 80s and 90s, you probably think of Marty McFly and his iconic moment in *Back To The Future*. Marty plays and sings lead with the house band on this song, while declaring afterward in reference to the "new sound" he introduced, "I guess you guys aren't ready for that, but your kids are gonna love it." When I hear this song, I have an interesting reaction. There is no admiration for Chuck Berry's trendsetting or nostalgia for teenage nights out at the movies. This song is a painful reminder of an inside joke my family used to play on me. It's the figurative representation of a life of growing up without the support and nurturing I needed, but it's also a reminder of how I still succeeded, even without a strong system of encouragement or support on which to depend.

My parents loved "Johnny Be Goode," especially my dad. We used to have a jukebox, and "Johnny" was in constant rotation. When I was about six years old and learning to ride my bike, my parents and siblings thought that it would be a good idea to encourage me by singing that song. I get that. "Go, Johnny! Go, go, go!" That seems innocent enough.

Well, what they soon discovered is that for some reason, hearing them sing that song made me nervous. The more they sang it, the more out of control my steering and balance would become. Eventually, I would get flustered and inevitably crash the bike. My family, upon seeing me crash, would burst into laughter. I would get up, dust myself off, and try again, and each time, the same thing would happen. I started riding, no training wheels back then, balance wobbly, but gaining stability. My family burst into song, "Go, Johnny, go, go, go!" There I went, into the back of a parked car, a tree, a ditch, or just down. It never failed. If they started singing that song, I would fall every single time, and every single time, they would laugh. After about the third or fourth cycle of trying to ride, my family singing that song, and then crashing into whatever mobile or immobile object in my path, I'd just drop my bike wherever I landed and run away. I usually ran into the woods, or sometimes into the house, while the family yelled, "We were just kidding. Stop! Come back!" Usually, when a child gives up like that, just walks away, it's a sign that they have lost a little faith in themselves and/or their abilities, and if things keep happening to push them to that point, they will one day lose confidence completely.

I'd be lying if I said that the interactions with my family didn't impact me. I still remember how much their amusement hurt my feelings. My chest got tight at the sound and sight of their laughter. I probably couldn't articulate to anyone what I was feeling at the time, but I do know now that I was feeling frustration, disappointment, humiliation, and anger. I was young, but I wasn't dumb. Not knowing exactly what I needed to help me was frustrating, but I knew their laughter wasn't helping. I started to realize that they were doing this on purpose, so I asked them, through my tears, to stop. "Please don't sing that song," to which they replied, "Oh, stop crying. Don't be a baby." What? I was a baby, a literal child, who was genuinely trying to accomplish a goal while my family, the closest people to me at the time, were actively using my pain for their amusement. One of the worst parts of this whole bike-riding humiliation is that they didn't just leave it there. This memory of me learning to ride the bike and crashing as a result of "Johnny Be Goode" became family lore for us. They just wouldn't let it go, adding insult to injury. When *Back to the Future* debuted in 1985, my dad went out and bought a DeLorean. After that, everyone commented about the song and made sure to ask if I remembered it and the circumstances around my learning to ride a bike. How could I forget? My family ruined that Chuck Berry song for me, and when I did finally see that scene in *Back To The Future* when Marty sings "Johnny Be Goode," I chuckled and cringed.

These bike-riding lessons were my first taste of disingenuous and inauthentic support, and my first realization that the tribe I was born into could be cruel. I don't know if they realized how hurtful their actions were. I now wonder if they knew how to genuinely support someone. It seems like the obvious action, while teaching me to ride a bike, would have been to hold the back of my seat while I rode or to show me how to slow down and brake properly, not finding every way to break my concentration, increase my anxiety, and make me fall. I knew something didn't feel right about what they were doing, but I wasn't aware that my family's reaction to me learning to ride my bike would become a harbinger of the support I would receive from them for the majority of my life. Whenever I would set my sights on a goal and bring it to my family's attention, I would either be met with no support at all or an invitation to call them when my efforts failed.

For a very long time, I would say up until the point that I married my husband at twenty-three, I kept waiting for my family's help and support, and I was disappointed every time. Consequently, one of the things that was important to me in marriage was finding someone who supported me. I made a vow to myself that I wanted to find someone who would finally step in and say, "We got this," instead of sitting idly wondering how something would play out with the expectation that failure was inevitable. Enter my husband Alex. If my parents and siblings are the prototype for how not to support a loved one, then my husband is the prototype for how to support a loved one. He shows up for me every day, but there's one particular memory that shows the contrast between his support and my family's. For context, you should know that before my husband and I became a couple, we were already best friends in college. Our friendship was like a parallel storyline to the relationship with my first fiancé, the same man who forcibly took my virginity. Alex knew many of the issues I had with my fiancé, so the groundwork and foundation for his support and being a person I could talk to when I was in distress and when I had something to celebrate was already there. When my family was nowhere to be found, I could go to Alex and say, "Oh, this good thing happened," and he wouldn't hesitate to celebrate with me. We studied together, worked on projects together, and had almost every class together. We registered together to make sure we were in the same classes.

When I was ready to end things with my fiancé, Alex was also there. Knowing that I, at least, had Alex's support, I mustered up enough courage to end my engagement. Everything was fine until the night my ex showed up at my apartment drunk. Still being fresh off the breakup, I was worried about him, so I brought him into my apartment, took care of him, and put him on the couch, where he eventually passed out. When he woke up the next morning, he had violence on his mind. He attacked me, beat the shit out of me. He even tried to go for my gun, which thankfully I had moved a couple of days before this happened. He looked for it in its original storage space and couldn't find it. This fight was bad, bar fight bad. Though he had a clear advantage over me, I fought with every ounce of energy I had. The whole time he was saying things like, "I'll hit you everywhere but the face, so nobody will see it. I'm going' kill you. Then, I'm going to kill myself." Not only was he beating up on me, but he also found the time to kick both my dog and my cat while this was going on. This man was on a rampage. At one point, he pinned me to the ground and began choking me. With his hands around my neck, he said something that sent shivers of fear through my bones. "I'm going to rape you. Then, I'm going to kill you, and it's your fault. You made me do this." That's when I realized that if I was going to survive this, I had to stop fighting back. From that moment on, I stopped fighting and just started repeating, "You're right. You're right. You're right." I got into the fetal position, put my hands on top of his hands as they were still around my neck, and just kept repeating, "You're right. You're right. You're right." Slowly, he began to come back to himself and took stock of what he was doing. He got off me and stormed angrily into the bathroom. While he was in there, I took my key off his keychain and put it in my pocket. He began yelling at me from the bathroom about wanting his engagement ring back, so I handed it back to him. All the while, I submissively answered, "You're right. You're right. You're right." I just kept saying that until he got himself together and left.

After finally getting him out of my apartment, I had a single moment of clarity in which I decided that I needed to change everything about my life so that he could never come back. I immediately took a shower to wash the stench of his anger off me, and made up my mind that I would not let him get away with this. I proceeded to figure out how I would tell my story because I knew that it was important to hold him accountable, but I was terrified. I told my family–my mom, my sister, and my brother. Their only question was, "Well, what did you do to make him do this?" I told a coworker, and he responded with, "You must've done something to set him off." These were people I thought I could trust. I was so disgusted with their responses that I felt like I would physically be sick. One person even remarked about how they didn't see any marks on me, which reminded me of what he said while he was beating me. That had been his point. My ex knew that people wouldn't believe me, so he intentionally avoided hitting me in easy-to-see areas to create doubt if I decided to tell. He thought of everything, and people were doing exactly what he knew they would do. There was one person, however, who didn't ask me any questions about what I did to provoke my ex. Alex. When I told him what happened, his only response was, "I'll be right over." The only question he did end up asking me was, "What do you need me to do?" to which I replied, "Just sit with me." That's what he did. He sat with me and supported me. I didn't report it to the police because I feared no one would believe me, and nothing would happen to him anyway. The only thing anyone suggested was that I move, change my locks, and/or get a bigger dog. To this day, I have PTSD as a result of this attack. Men can't stand too close behind me or between me and the exit in a menacing way. They can't make certain motions or gestures around me or surprise me. I can't handle people touching my neck because I revert to that feeling of being asphyxiated. Alex lives with me every day, knowing that the scarring that man left on me is permanent. He still shows up for me, and his unwavering love and support have shown me the difference between genuine support and inauthentic support, the kind my family offered.

Even now, after all these years, my family's lack of support for me is still a sensitive subject. I wish I could say it's gotten better, but it hasn't. I had the honor of doing a TEDx Talk a while ago. It was one of the most amazing moments of my life. My family has yet to even acknowledge that I did it. I've shared other achievements like the TEDx Talk with them and gotten crickets. When I experience loss or disappointment, though, the conversation is incessant. A few years ago, we lost our beach house in a hurricane. My family had much to say about that. The comments were reminiscent of that same attitude that always accompanies their discussions of "Johnny Be Goode". "Oh, I heard you lost the beach house. Are you okay? I'm so sorry you lost everything. I'm so sorry everything was ruined. How will you cope?" If one didn't know my family history, one might be inclined to believe that there was genuine concern there. However, none of those questions were followed up with, "What can I do to help?"

Though I've come to expect this kind of treatment and those kinds of responses from them, it still stings. I try not to lean into the negative thoughts concerning this and their continued lack of support, but I'm still working through the insecurity of not feeling encouraged or championed by my family. It's an ongoing healing process. In the meantime, though, my family's habitual indifference concerning me has benefited me and my community by teaching me how to be intentional about the ways I show up for others. If someone reaches out to me for help, my response is usually, "I'm there. What do you need?" I've helped people who have found themselves rejected by their parents. I've held people's hands who've had to make devastating family decisions. I have never said no to a flare for help that's gone up. I don't care where I am or what time it is. It could be two in the morning, and I'm going to do what I can to help because I remember the sensations of what it felt like not to have that. There's nothing more acutely painful than crying out for help and watching someone you love, and who you thought loved you, turn away. That very feeling pushed me to make the decision, as long as I'm able, I will help whenever I can. No flare that I see will go unanswered.

My family's disinterest in showing up for me in a real way also exposed me to how people can feign support for each other. There is a difference between cheering someone on authentically and sarcastically, and I think that sometimes we say, "You can do this," and mean it. Other times we say, "You can do this", and we're being cynical and inauthentic. Authenticity, when supporting people, is important. Performative support and motivation might just be worse than no support at all because it's a facade of care and encouragement concealing the desire to see someone fail. In my experience, when people offer that kind of inauthentic support, it's for a myriad of reasons. It's either to show intellectual or moral superiority or to come in and save someone, so the person offering support looks like the hero. Whatever the motivation behind the inauthenticity, people know the difference, so don't try to be there for people if you're not being authentic. Don't be there to rescue them. Don't be there to watch them fall. Don't be there to prove a point. Be there because you love them. Be there because you genuinely want to see them succeed.

How many people in your life show you that kind of inauthentic support, or worse, are you that person in someone else's life? Do you find yourself saying things like, "I can't wait for that to blow up. Are you sure that's a good idea? I don't know. Call me if you have a problem," to people that you care about when they're trying something new or pursuing a goal? What are you saying to that person? Do you believe in them? Are you motivating them? Are you supporting them? Authentic support requires empathy and not sympathy. According to Brene Brown, there is a stark difference. "Empathy fuels connection while sympathy drives disconnection. Empathy is 'I'm feeling with you.' Sympathy, 'I'm feeling for you.'" When we present ourselves as support for our loved ones, we need to examine whether we're being sympathetic or empathetic, whether we're coming alongside them, being what they need at the moment, or observing from a comfortable distance, making declarations of the obvious, to make ourselves feel better. I'm not sure what the end goal was for my family when they decided to taunt me with "Johnny Be Goode". However, the person that I am as a result of their lack of support would handle that situation very differently. If someone thinks enough of me to solicit help for riding the metaphorical bike, I'm leaning in to help. I'll spend as long as it takes holding the back of that seat, watching out for cars, making sure their nerves are calm, and that they feel safe. I will throw myself on top of the curb before they fall to lessen the impact. I will do whatever it takes until they can ride that bike without complaint and worry because I've been there and genuinely want to help. That is what empathy looks like when providing support. In all reality, had my folks been more supportive of me, I'm not sure I would know how to genuinely show up for others in the way that I do. In their way, they helped make me better for those who might need me.

Another unintentional lesson I learned from this reality that no one was coming to save me, is that my spirit is indomitable, and my determination, relentless. I have had to overcome so many things in my life, many of which I mention in this book. Had there been access to a soft place to land early on, I may not have developed the self-reliance and confidence needed to survive and thrive through all of those things. By no means am I justifying the abandonment I experienced from my family, but I acknowledge that it made me stronger. There were doors that I needed to open that required me to be confident enough in my abilities to open those doors, whether I had the support or not. I'm proud of that, and I know that the fortitude with which I was able to accomplish those goals was a direct result of my having to figure things out on my own. I say all of that to emphasize the fact that, despite who does or doesn't show up in support of your endeavors, you must reach down deep inside and find the courage to show up for yourself. Once you do, and you realize that you are capable beyond your limitations or circumstances, that confidence will grow, and you'll find that you can succeed whether friends, family, colleagues, or anybody is there to support you. That's the lesson.

Canine Sadness

I am a dog—I have no purpose other than servitude
My lifelong task—to love and accept my master
My life clings to her every word—Shall I get fed? Shall I
* be protected?*

My fur is soft and shiny—it catches the sunlight
My noble eyes are the color of the sea—where shallow
* meets deep*
I can see far into my master's soul—she cannot fool me

I can hear with my fluffy pointed ears
I can listen with my special sense
My master's moods are easily understood—time to
* sleep, play or fetch?*

I take her punishment with a soft whimper
I wish I could speak my feelings to her
I accept and love—judgement is left to humans

October 24, 1988

10

....

CANIS VITA EST

The universe has a way of speaking to us. I believe that whatever force is out there constantly communicates with us through signs, nature, animals, etc. Every pivotal moment of my life has involved a canine. I don't remember a time in my life when I haven't had a dog. Regarding the number of nights I have not slept with the dog, it's probably less than two months. I connect with nature in general, but I have a real affinity for anything that's canine. They have been like angels on this planet for me. I've always connected with them. I've always thought that if it hadn't been for dogs at different points in my life, things would have happened very differently for me. When I was a child wandering around in the woods while my family had no idea where I was, I never wandered without a dog by my side. I've always had large dogs, except for the little Frenchie I have now, and they've always accompanied me for protection and companionship. When I think about those Ted Bundy years, I think of how there could have been flyers posted around town about my abduction, pictures of a thirteen-year-old who could've been mistaken for sixteen or seventeen. However, it's much harder to take someone who has an 80-pound shepherd mix walking right beside her. Not saying a criminally minded person with bad intentions wouldn't have tried to harm me, simply because a dog was present, but I think they would think a little longer about doing anything with a healthy canine companion tagging along with their suspected target.

For example, there was a time in Miami, Florida, when I'm positive that I was going to be abducted. Positive. I was jogging alone, headphones on. They were corded back in the day, which doesn't make a difference, other than to make you aware of the time. I soon noticed a white van pulling up beside me, and it eventually stopped. I did not feel good about it at all. The guys were looking for an address, and something about them gave me the heebie-jeebies. It was a "proverbial" white rape van in every way possible way. When I say I was jogging alone, I mean no other people were jogging with me. I did, however, have my Akita—St. Bernard mix rescue named Gorky with me. This dog was massive, and luckily for me at the time, he wasn't nice to anyone but me. The guys in the van noticed that immediately because as they pulled up, my dog went apeshit. They asked me where a particular address was, and I strategically put the dog between the van and me and answered that I didn't know where it was. The men replied, "Ok," and they drove off. I kept going, but my dog just would not settle down. I kept seeing the van at different parts of my walk, and I thought, *This is bad.* The dog was still going crazy, and I began to worry that they might come up behind me and do something to the dog. In an attempt to throw them off, I started walking toward areas that were a little more populated. When that didn't work, I spotted a house that had security cameras and looked secure and different, pretended that was my house, went around back, jumped a fence, and hung out on that back porch long enough for the van to lose enough patience and interest in me to leave. Thankfully, they did finally give up and leave. As I re-emerged from the strangers' back porch, I breathed a sigh of relief and gratitude for my dog's protection. It wasn't just the fact that he bared his teeth, barked, and growled at my would-be assailants, but it was my dog's strange behavior in the presence of the van that first made me aware of their ominous presence. Gorky's alertness is what made me check my surroundings and take my headphones off to be fully aware of my surroundings. I'm not sure that day would have proceeded as I described had Gorky not been there.

In addition to protecting me from people, my dogs have also protected me from other animals. There were plenty of times when I would wander around in the woods and eventually end up in the pasture with the cows. Cows can be sweet, but bulls, not so much. One day, no doubt during one of my many meandering nature walks surrounding my house in North Florida, I found myself face to face with a bull. Thankfully, I had a dog with me that sensed the danger in this situation and instinctively got between me and the bull, giving me enough time to go hide behind a tree and avoid being killed or at least severely gouged by the bull. Granted, I had no business in that pasture, but I'm so grateful that the dog was there, not just for companionship, but protection.

In my young adult life, I had to deal with a "peeping Tom" situation. I was advised by police to get a large dog for added protection in case my stalker decided to escalate and harm me in the future. I took their advice and got a Rottweiler puppy that I named Lady Isabeau d'Anjou—we called her Isabeau. The relationship with that dog was the most powerful example of the special connection I have with canines. I trained her to protect me, and she became an amazing protector. She was there for many milestones in my adulthood. She was with me through the beginning of my relationship with my now husband. She was with me through the birth of my daughter. She was the first one to meet the baby when we got home from the hospital. She probably knew I was pregnant before I knew I was pregnant. She immediately started sniffing my belly and knew there was a baby in there. When the baby was awake and hungry, she was the first to notify us. Isabeau sat by me for all the nighttime feedings. I would hold the baby during feedings, and she would lie down on the couch and put her head under the baby's. You could not approach the baby without her sniffing you out and verifying if you were okay to be around the baby. If I put the baby in the front yard to play, Isabeau put herself between the road and the baby. She loved the baby; she loved me, and I loved her. When she began to get sick, we knew the end was near. I didn't want her to suffer, so I told her, " Give me a sign that you want me to let you go without suffering." I made a deal with her that if she went three days without touching food, then I would know that she wanted me to let her go. I spent the next three days tempting her with everything she loved: hot dogs, cheese, and whipped cream. For three whole days, she didn't touch a morsel of any food, so I knew it was time. We made the appointment with the vet and let the kids say goodbye. The kids didn't really understand what was going on, but they hugged her and made their peace as much as possible. We let her go peacefully and quietly under a tree. It was quite beautiful.

Soon after her passing, I had to take a business trip to Mexico. I still didn't know if it had been the right decision to let my dog go when I did. I was still really struggling with whether she had more time or not. She had Addison's disorder, among other issues, which is an endocrine disorder that occurs when dogs' adrenal glands fail to produce the hormones they need. I had been going back and forth with the universe about whether I had done the right thing because I didn't want her to suffer, but I also didn't want to feel like we robbed her of time she could have had here as well. As I arrived in Mexico, all these questions were on my mind. My boss and I arrived in this small town in the middle of nowhere, Mexico, and our hosts told us that before we got down to business, they wanted to take us on a tour of this famous chapel in town dedicated to St. Dominic. It is important to note that I was also serving as interpreter on this trip for my boss. Before the tour started, I was standing behind my boss, over his shoulder, and our guides told me to translate for him. We went into this chapel, and they immediately started talking about Saint Dominic. St. Dominic is frequently depicted in art with a dog because when his mother was pregnant with him, she dreamt of a big, large dog with a torch in his mouth that gave her this joyous news that she would soon give birth to a baby boy. The tour guide further discussed how her son grew up to become a priest who was always surrounded by dogs. This particular priest founded the Dominican order and did some great things, but the part of the story that was so obviously resonating with me was how it related to dogs—the name of the order itself came from the Latin words for "holy dog". As I looked around the church, I noticed that there were dogs included in the decorations all over the church. They were everywhere. There had to be at least 25,000 representations of dogs in that building. That is not an exaggeration. I was translating and crying the entire time. I'm sure my boss thought I was having some kind of religious experience, and I was, just not in the way he was thinking.

At that moment, I realized that the universe was giving me a sign that I had done the right thing when it came to Isabeau. The overwhelming presence of dogs in this building, in the pews, in the pillars, on the windows, they were all a reminder of my sweet pup. This feeling of certainty overcame me, and I thought about how beautiful and amazing the universe is. I understood something universal at that moment. No matter where you go, and no matter what you call him or her, there is something bigger than all of us. Every culture has a name for it; every group of people has a different story about it, and every single version has some truth in it. If you just open yourself up, you're going to receive messages and you're going to receive signs. I asked the universe if I had made the right decision by not having to watch this beloved part of nature, a companion that had protected and comforted me her whole life, die a slow and horrible death. I decided to put her to sleep without pain before her organs shut down, suffocating her to death. I was unsure of my decision. I asked for a sign confirming it was the right thing to do, and the signs slapped me in the face by way of this beautiful cathedral in the middle of nowhere, Mexico, and it was glorious.

"Canis vita est," is Latin for "dogs are life," and the experience I had in that Mexican cathedral confirmed that very idea for me, as well as the belief that everybody has a spirit animal. In different cultures and belief systems, people recognize the human-to-animal connection, even if they can't explain it. The animal could be a wolf, an owl, a dragonfly, a snake, or anything. Regardless of the animal, the connection is what's important. For whatever reason, the universe chose to connect me with dogs, and that relationship has taught me not to miss the signs. If you are blessed enough to have a special connection with an animal, cherish it. The universe is always communicating with us, whether it be through animals, plants, the weather, or any other natural phenomena. The signs are always there. If we pay attention, they can help us find peace, comfort, understanding, and confirmation for many of the questions and challenges we face. We just have to be open to receiving the messages. That's the lesson.

Now

If you do not know—learn more

If you cannot see—look closer

If you cannot hear—listen intently

If you cannot manage—change now

September 8, 1986

11

....

A LITTLE GIFT FROM JANE

Everyone has a memory or two that makes such an impact that they try to incorporate the lessons learned from that into everyday decisions. One such event happened for me in my early twenties. I was just starting out on my own and had just barely avoided being homeless. I had just gotten an apartment, and all I could afford was the rent. I had no furniture and nothing else to decorate or make my little apartment a home. I had to get creative with my decor, so in the absence of a real table, I put a glass top that I found on the side of the road on top of some milk crates to make a table. This was just one of the many accommodations I made to compensate for my lack of funds. Months later, Jane, my boss at the time, became aware of my situation and offered to help. She had a storage unit full of furniture and other household items left over from her last move. One day, she handed me the key to her storage unit and said, "Here's the key to the storage unit. I want you to take everything there that is useful to you and make your apartment a home. Whatever items you don't need, though, you have to find someone else who can use them." She required that I pay her kindness forward by giving someone else the things I didn't use.

Going into that storage room was heaven for me because no one else had helped me up until that point, even though many people in my life were aware of the conditions in which I was living. In fact, someone had helped me find a sofa, but they charged me $200 for it. Another person had been willing to allow me to live in their spare guest den, but then charged me $300 a month and housekeeping services to stay there. I went into that storage room with gratitude and excitement. Since Jane was single at the time, there was just enough for another bachelorette pad. Everything was mismatched, but I managed to get at least four of each of the essentials I needed—four plates, four cups, and an actual dining room table with chairs. I was elated! I spent the rest of my time there crying and packing up the things I needed, overflowing with gratitude for my boss showing me that people can show up and support each other. I got everything I needed, and for the rest, anytime I saw somebody who looked like or mentioned they might need some household items, I offered what was left of my boss's things to them.

I never forgot Jane's kindness to me during that time. Ever since that moment, I've made it a point to make sure I spread the same kind of generosity to others that Jane showed me. I even practiced this habit with my children. Every six months or so, I put a box or a bag in the middle of their room and said, "Everything we don't want to play with anymore, everything we no longer need, it's time to donate." We have tried to pay it forward every year for the holidays. We adopted families from Habitat for Humanity, and we gave them everything they wanted for Christmas. Every time there is anything we don't want, we find a new home for it. We pay it forward, and I think that's one of the lessons Jane taught me back then. If there is something you have that can bring someone else joy, why not give it to them? I have kept that ideology going to this day, no matter how big or small. What Jane did for me was huge, but not every situation has to be that impactful. I've found more opportunities to do small things for people over the years.

Many years after my dream shopping trip to Jane's storage unit, I had this handcrafted necklace that I found at an art show. I wore it to work quite often, and I had one coworker who would comment, " I just love that necklace. I love that necklace," every time I would wear it. Subconsciously, I made a note that she loved the necklace. I wore the necklace to work again, and just like clockwork, my coworker replied, "I just love that necklace!" At that moment, the memory of Jane kicked in, and I said, "Wait! Wait! Come back!" I unclasped the necklace from my neck and immediately re-clasped it around hers. She got teary-eyed and adamantly refused, but I declared, " You always mention it. You do love it, and I think it brings you more joy than it brings me. So you should have it." My coworker was astonished that I did that, but I explained to her what was done for me when I was younger and how I want to share that lesson of kindness with others. I also told her what I always tell people when they ask me why I do things like this. My first response is always that I help because someone helped me. My only requirement when I do help is that the person returns the favor and pays it forward. I believe that when that right time comes, each person will know it. Paying it forward is how we return kindness to the universe. That's the lesson.

Wonder About Me

I lie in the dreams of many
So many dream to be like me
Yet still I guard my essence

I am beauty, yet I am plain
I am soft, yet am I unmoving
Call me woman, I have many names

No one can be the perfect me
Never can all fit me exactly
I am now, yet am I eternity

In my eyes, see all the women before me
They melt, and mold, and configure
Into the women of tomorrow

Mine is the soul with room for addition
Mine is the body that bears the ripeness
Mine is the heart that overruns its boundaries

I am the celebration of man
It is in me, that his joys become souls
I hold the womb that is the future

Man cannot define me, my true definitions
Number as the streetlights on a horizon
Thousands, or not a single one

I am she, me, and all of the world
The power is mine to make myself over
And over, and over

I have broken the confines that once held me
Yesterday, I was enslaved by others
Today, my only master is myself

My essence is in the reflection of my mind
I am that which I choose to be
Seek not my meaning, but that which I show you

My mystery, my essence is in that
That which you cannot and should not know
So wonder on

1992

CONCLUSION

The idea of me being the milkman's daughter haunted me for most of my life. Though my family seemed to be intent on turning my uniqueness into the joke of my illegitimacy, the truth is I am not the milkman's daughter. I am my father's daughter. I'm proud to be my father's daughter, not because I'm like him, but because of him and despite him, I am a good person. I choose to be good, and I choose to do good every day. That doesn't mean I'm perfect or always make the right choices—but I try to stay true to myself. With all the unflattering stories told about my birth, I believe the timing of my life is special. Every experience I've had has put me on the path to make the choices I've made, and to answer the rescue flares that have been released. Each challenge I overcame emboldened me to try to help others, so they don't have to feel or experience any of the negativity I felt and experienced.

The fact that I can even write this book about my life and the difficulties of my past is evidence that I'm a survivor. I'm proof that terrible things can happen, but they don't have to be all-consuming. There is healing on the other side of tragedy, hurt, and trauma, but we have to choose it. We're all faced with that choice daily. Do we repeat the sins of our fathers, mothers, sisters, brothers, or whoever was charged with nurturing us into maturity, or do we choose to break generational traumas? Do we choose to let the incidents that have hurt or impacted us in negative ways color our perception of the human experience negatively, or do we accept that we can't change the past and move forward with the knowledge that no pain is futile? You can extract certain personal truths and ideologies from your lived experience to help you form the guardrails for your life. You can then use those guardrails to guide you into better decisions that will impact not just you, but everyone you touch.

I challenge you to look for those moments, those decisions that might cause a ripple effect that will influence someone's life for the better. They may not be giant, "Aha," larger-than-life, hero moments. Yes, some people encounter those opportunities, every once in a while, but I'm referencing those smaller, heroic micro moments. Tuesday, you might open the door for someone, and on Friday, you compliment someone's appearance, which starts the whole ripple effect of them having a great day and doing great things. Then the next week, you listen to someone who's having a hard day, and that quiets the whispers of suicide that have been floating around their thoughts. If you're looking for your purpose, what could be more beautiful than that? That's why I survived, and the same can be true for you. Part of our job as members of this global community is to perform these micro acts of kindness and rescue, leading with compassion, empathy, and love. I try to live this every day. That's part of my motivation for writing this book. Everyone's method of fulfilling their purpose will be different, but the power of all of us to positively, energetically perform daily acts of kindness can shift the planet, making all that we've experienced, all that we survived, worth it. We are powerful, and life teaches me that every day. That's the lesson.

ACKNOWLEDGEMENTS

To Misha Bleymaier-Farrish—Thank you for believing that I could "Get this shit done!"

To Alacia Reynolds—A very special thank you and heartfelt appreciation. These words do not exist without you. You are amazing, and your questions and patience with me were profound. Now get out of my head!

To my Besties, Becca, Lourdes, Deanna, and Anacielo—Thank you for holding space for me while I contemplated this book, stressed over it, and lived the lessons I write about in this book in real life.

To my family—Daddy, Mom, Deysi, Victor (and from all the different corners of my family tree)—I love you all, and thank you for teaching me to recognize my own strength.

Most importantly, to my beloveds, Alex, Lauren & Marc, and David—Thank you for always standing with me. You are all the reasons for my happiness, and that my lessons matter.

ABOUT THE COVER

The cover design is based on images from a unique therapy session I went through at TheraPaint Studio in Nashville, Tennessee founded by a wonderful soul named Jackie Laurian Long.

TheraPaint Studio, a first-of-its-kind wellness concept, is redefining emotional healing through the act of throwing paint. Nestled in a serene, spa-like environment, TheraPaint offers individuals and small groups the opportunity to release and process emotions freely in a non-clinical setting. Every completed artwork is composted on-site, transforming released energy into new growth within the studio's peaceful garden. Through individual sessions, community events, and curated offerings, TheraPaint Studio creates a safe, beautiful space for therapeutic renewal from the inside out.

To learn more or schedule a session if you are visiting Nashville, please scan here:

It is important to find every resource available to you for connecting with ways to heal and finding your voice. No matter where you are in the world—breathe, connect, listen, heal, and pay it forward.

ABOUT THE AUTHOR

Yesi B. Sevilla, a TEDx speaker, has more than twenty years of experience in leadership roles across varying industries, including educational technology, global biotechnology, healthcare, consulting, and post-secondary education. Her diverse industry background, global business acumen, and dedication to inclusive innovation make her an invaluable resource in innovating, collaborating, building, and leading. Not only is Yesi an accomplished professional, but she also lives a full life as a wife, mother, sister, friend, mentor, and lover of nature. Yesi has always been an avid reader and language enthusiast, evidenced by her ability to speak, read, and write fluently in English and Spanish and conversationally in Portuguese. Yesi has a passion to help and support others in whatever way she can, whether through mentoring, sharing her time and resources with local organizations, or just providing a listening ear to a loved one. That same passion was one of the main motivators to write *The Milkman's Daughter—Lessons From My Life's Early Memories*.

Yesi believes that the lessons she learned from experiences in her youth and young adulthood created the foundation for her current beliefs and values. After reflecting on situations from her past, both good and bad, and through years of therapy and other healing work, Yesi has realized that her past experiences served as lessons to guide her in the present. In this book, Yesi shares intimate details of her life with candor and transparency to address a range of topics from childhood neglect to religion, sexual agency, and more. This literary offering is not just a recounting of personal events, but it is also an exercise in self-reflection. With each memory, Yesi details the lessons she learned, providing an opportunity for the reader to reflect on his or her memories and make conclusions about the lessons of such memories. The book shows that every trial, tribulation, and triumph we endure has value. Audiences can expect to be inspired and challenged to see their experiences as opportunities for learning, growth, and development for their current and future belief systems.